Colenso 1899

The Boer War In Natal

Campaign • 38

Colenso 1899

The Boer War In Natal

Ian Knight

Series editor Lee Johnson • *Consultant editor* David G Chandler

First published in Great Britain in 1995 by Osprey Publishing,
Midland House, West Way, Botley, Oxford OX2 0PH, UK
44-02 23rd St, Suite 219, Long Island City, NY 11101, USA
E-mail: info@ospreypublishing.com

Transferred to digital print on demand 2010

First published 1995
1st impression 1995

Printed and bound by PrintOnDemand-Worldwide.com Peterborough, UK

A CIP catalogue record for this book is available from the British Library

ISBN: 978 1 85532 466 4

Military Editor: Lee Johnson
Edited by Tony Holmes
Design by Paul Kime
Colour bird's-eye view illustrations by Peter Harper
Maps by Micromap
Wargaming *Colenso* and *Spioenkop* by Ian Knight
Filmset in Great Britain

Dedication
To Rick Scollins, whose sad and untimely death in December 1992 prevented 'the old team' working together again on this one,
as we had planned.

Author's note
I'd like to express my thanks to all those who have helped in the preparation of this book, particularly Gilbert Torlage, of the Natal
Museums' Service, who gave up several days of his free time to take me around the Colenso, Spioenkop and Thukela Heights battlefields, on which he is an expert. My old friend 'SB' Bourquin made free with his incomparable photographic collection once more, and
all of the musuems, both in the UK and South Africa, with whom I came into contact, were unfailingly helpful. The decision to use the
Afrikaans spelling *Spioenkop*, rather than the anglicised version, *Spion Kop*, is the result of a purely personal preference on my part
for rendering South African place-names accordinig to the language in which they were titled. Hence also the technically more correct
Thukela, rather than the more familiar *Tugela*, and *Mafikeng* rather than *Mafeking*.

The Woodland Trust
Osprey Publishing is supporting the Woodland Trust, the UK's leading woodland conservation charity, by funding
the dedication of trees.

www.ospreypublishing.com

Key to military series symbols

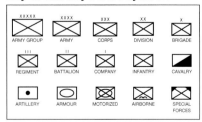

CONTENTS

THE ORIGINS OF THE ANGLO-BOER WAR 7

OPPOSING STRATEGIES AND ARMIES 12
The Boers · The British

THE NATAL CAMPAIGN – THE OPENING STAGES 31
The Prelude to Colenso

THE COMMANDERS 36

THE BATTLE OF COLENSO 40

THE AFTERMATH OF COLENSO 56

THE BATTLE OF SPIOENKOP 64
After Spioenkop

BREAKTHROUGH 80
The Relief of Ladysmith

THE BATTLEFIELDS TODAY 86

CHRONOLOGY 91

A GUIDE TO FURTHER READING 93

WARGAMING COLENSO AND SPIOENKOP 95

THE ORIGINS OF
THE ANGLO-BOER WAR

President Paul Kruger of the South African Republic (Transvaal); he was a bitter opponent of British interference in the affairs of the Boer republics.

LEFT *Commandant Schalk Burger, who commanded the Twin Peaks sector during the attack on Spioenkop.*

In 1899 Great Britain was at the height of its Imperial power. The Queen Empress had been on the throne for more than 50 glittering years, and her domain touched upon every continent. Yet, even at this very pinnacle of Imperial pomp and majesty, the British army, the guardian of Empire in countless wars across the globe, was destined to be humiliated by poorly-organised citizen militia consisting of men whom the British professionals despised as back-woods farmers. In one week in December 1899 the farmers of the South African Boer republics of the Orange Free State and the Transvaal inflicted three serious reverses on British troops. In the hills around Stormberg railway junction, on the dusty plain before the Magersfontein heights, and on the grassy flats before the Thukela heights at Colenso, the highly trained British military machine ground to a halt in the face of the Boers' practised marksmanship and fieldcraft. The shock waves of this 'Black Week' reverberated around the Empire, for the action at Colenso involved not merely a military reverse, but the humiliation of a national hero. Worse, it was the precursor of some of the toughest fighting Britain had experienced since the Crimean War.

South Africa had long been a source of irritation to the British Colonial Office, and the events which brought British and Boer forces into open confrontation were merely the climax to nearly a century of mutual antagonism. Europeans had first come to the Cape in 1652, when the Dutch East India Company established a way-station at the extreme southern tip of the continent. Africa itself held little interest to the emerging European empires, but the Cape commanded the long sea route to the Indies, where the real profits lay. The Company steadfastly refused the responsibility of developing its African possessions, but it did allow its employees to establish small-holdings to grow produce for the ships. Over the next century, these frontier farmers developed an independence and toughness of spirit which refused to be contained by the Company's boundaries, and European settlement gradually crept away from the Cape's formal border and into the interior. In time these Dutch farmers, augmented by a trickle of French and German religious refugees from Europe, developed their own local dialect, and a decidedly African outlook, and began to think of themselves as a distinct race, the Afrikaners – white Africans.

The British first arrived at the Cape in the late eighteenth century,

ABOVE *Piet Joubert (seated centre right with beard) and his commandants in the field early in the Natal campaign. On active service Boer commanders were largely indistinguishable from their men.*

RIGHT *A Boer commando mustering on the eve of the war.*

when, during the political twists and turns which characterised the Napoleonic Wars, they found themselves fighting the Dutch. Their administration became permanent in 1806, but whilst their interests, too, were primarily those of world strategy, their administration soon antagonised the *Boere burghers* – the Boer farmers. By this time the eastern fringes of the expanding Boer society had become locked in a bitter struggle with local African groups for possession of the land, and the Boers deeply resented the apparently even-handed attitude that the British promulgated on the frontier.

When the British abolished slavery, on which many Boers depended for their work-force, many Boers concluded that they simply could not live under British rule. In the 1830s an exodus known as the Great Trek began. The Trekkers aimed to open up lands in the south African interior where they could live without interference, and their progress was marked by a conflict with both the African groups who owned the land before them, and with the British, who haphazardly tried to block their progress. In 1842 a British expeditionary force drove the Boers from Port Natal – later Durban – and seized the eastern seaboard for the Crown. Further fighting over the next few years initially secured territory north of the Orange River for Britain, but by the 1850s Britain abandoned its claims to the interior. By the end of the decade, therefore, Britain held the Cape and Natal, whilst the Boers had established two republics inland – the Orange Free State and the South African Republic, known as the Transvaal. Caught between these twin grindstones, the indigenous black groups suffered a steady loss of independence and territory.

The subsequent decades were, nonetheless, marked by a jockeying for power between the two white groups. The Transvaal was keen to open a route to the sea and advance north of the Limpopo river, but lacked the resources to confront the African kingdoms which blocked their path. In the 1870s, the British Colonial Office, tired of the incessant bickering in southern Africa, and spurred on by the recent discovery of diamonds at Kimberley, adopted a forward policy known as Confederation. This was simply a scheme to bring together the different groups across the region under British dominion so as to facilitate economic development. Since by this time the Transvaal Government was bankrupt and under threat from its Zulu neighbours, Britain audaciously stepped in and annexed the Republic in 1877 as the first step in its plan. A quick war against the Zulus was supposed to follow, but when this turned into a costly slogging match, the Home Government abandoned the Confederation policy. The Transvaal burghers waited until the Zulus had been defeated, then rose up against the British administration. The British force sent to suppress them suffered a series of reverses culminating in the humiliating defeat at Majuba on 26 February 1881, in which the British General, Sir George Colley, was himself killed. A hastily negotiated peace allowed Britain to withdraw from the Transvaal whilst still retaining a nominal claim to suzerainty; this 'peace without honour' was bitterly resented by both British settlers in South Africa and many in the army. 'Remember Majuba!' was to prove a potent rallying cry in the years to come.

Piet Joubert in the uniform of Commandant-General of the Transvaal. Joubert was a hero of the 1881 Transvaal War, but by 1899 he had become slow and over-cautious.

The Transvaal might have enjoyed its independence indefinitely, had not its economic position been redefined by the discovery of gold at the Witwatersrand in 1886, just 5 years after Majuba. This, coming on top of the discovery of diamonds at Kimberley, suggested that southern Africa might include some of the world's richest natural resources. The discoveries attracted the attention of powerful British entrepreneurs and empire-builders, and by the 1890s a 'forward policy' was once again in the air. Many of the foreign miners and craftsmen who flooded to the Witwatersrand gold workings, and to the burgeoning town of Johannesburg, were British in origin, yet the Transvaal Republic steadfastly refused to grant them anything more than minimal political rights. To President Paul Kruger, a hard-line republican who as a boy had lived through the Great Trek, these men were *uitlanders* – foreigners – who must expect to trade the heavy taxes the Transvaal levied on them against their gold profits, and who had no right to expect to vote. Since the *uitlanders* soon came to outnumber the Boers in the Transvaal, Kruger insisted that to offer them the franchise was tantamount to hauling down the Boer flag over the capital, Pretoria. This was an attitude which infuriated mining magnates like Cecil Rhodes, whose huge personal fortune was based on diamonds and gold, who wielded tremendous political power, and who dreamt one day of building a British railway all the way from the Cape to Cairo. Rhodes had already organised the settlement of the territory north of the Transvaal – for 80 years it was known as Rhodesia – and towards the end of 1895 he attempted to mount a coup to over-throw Kruger's regime.

The attempt proved a fiasco. Rhodes' plan was to send a column of volunteers into Johannesburg under the command of his lieutenant, Dr

Leander Starr Jameson, to precipitate a rising by the oppressed *uitlanders*. In the event the *uitlanders* proved unwilling to rise, and Jameson's men were surrounded and arrested after a fight at a spot not far from Johannesburg called Doornkop.

The Jameson Raid was a major step on the road to the Anglo-Boer War. It raised the level of political tension and suspicion between the Transvaal and Britain, whilst at the same time highlighting the *uitlander* issue and the role of Rhodes and his capitalist clique, the so-called 'goldbugs'. A new High Commissioner, sent by the Colonial Office to the Cape in the aftermath of the Raid, Sir Alfred Milner, firmly believed that the situation could only be resolved by confrontation with the Transvaal, and, despite the more cautious attitude of his superiors in London, began to work towards an open rift. In the Transvaal President Kruger refused to budge on the *uitlander* question, and began to import arms from Europe in expectation of conflict. The Orange Free State, although not directly involved in these wrangles, agreed to support its northern neighbour in the event of war. In June 1899 Milner and Kruger met at Bloemfontein, the Free State capital, to try to negotiate a settlement, but neither side had much to gain by compromise. Milner broke off negotiations, and by September the *uitlanders* were fleeing the Transvaal in droves, taking refuge in the British colonies, the Cape and Natal. In this atmosphere of heightened tension, British troops already in South Africa were moved towards vulnerable towns on the borders. At home, the British government authorised the despatch of further troops to South Africa, and Kruger, in an attempt to seize the initiative before they arrived, issued an ultimatum demanding the withdrawal of soldiers from the borders. It expired on 11 October 1899, and the Anglo-Boer War, known to the Afrikaners as the *Tweede Vryheidsoorlog* (the 'second war of freedom'), began.

OPPOSING STRATEGIES AND ARMIES

At the outbreak of hostilities, the combined forces of the two Boer republics amounted to little more than 40,000 men. Although these included small professional contingents in both armies, the bulk were essentially a civilian militia. Since the total was only more or less equivalent to the British reinforcements by then on the high seas, the Republics decided to opt for an aggressive strategy. With Majuba very much in mind, they hoped to strike swiftly at the existing British garrisons, inflict on them defeats sufficient to drag them to the negotiating table, and then conclude a political settlement before Britain could bring her full might to bear.

This invasion took place across several fronts. In the west, the British had secured Kimberley in the northern Cape, and Mafikeng, further north, which commanded the road to Rhodesia. By threatening these dusty frontier towns the Boers could strike at the basis of British economic interests in the region. Both were quickly surrounded and invested, but the Boers were unwilling to risk the heavy cost that would inevitably accompany any attempt to take them by storm. A third Boer thrust was made into the northern Cape in an attempt to provoke a rising of those Afrikaners who still lived under British rule in the colonies. By far the biggest thrust, however, came in the east, where the Transvaal's main forces, led by Commandant General Piet Joubert, and supported by several Free State commandos, crossed the Drakensberg mountain passes, under the very shadow of Majuba, and struck into Natal.

Despite the years of tension which preceded it, the outbreak of hostilities found the British army singularly unprepared. The British commander on the spot, Sir William Butler, had steadfastly refused to admit the inevitability of conflict, and so had refused to make contingency plans. He was subsequently replaced, and his successor, General Penn-Symons, was of a more aggressive state of mind, but Britain had scarcely 10,000 troops in South Africa when the Boer invasion began. The Commander-in-Chief in London, Sir Garnet Wolseley, urged the government to mobilise the Army and its reserve immediately, but Wolseley, once the thrusting 'very model of a modern Major-General', was losing his health and his influence, whilst the army was riven by petty jealousies at the highest level, and the government itself hesitated to take drastic action. It took several weeks for an 'Army Corps' to be raised at home, and in the meantime troops were

Lieutenant-General Sir George White (seated centre, in hat) and his staff, photographed in Ladysmith during the siege.

despatched to South Africa from India as a stop-gap. Whilst he waited for them to arrive, Penn-Symons planned to check the Boer advance below the Drakensberg foothills, before it could threaten the main settler towns further south.

OPPOSING ARMIES

THE BOERS

The Boers who streamed into the British colonies in October 1899 were citizen soldiers. Neither the Transvaal nor the Free State possessed more than a handful of regular troops, and the cornerstone of their military system remained the commando. The commando system dated back to the early Boer experience on the Cape Frontier, and it imposed an obligation on any male capable of bearing arms to turn out armed and equipped at his own expense when the occasion demanded. Traditionally, this included all men between the ages of 16 and 60, although men in the prime of life were naturally preferred if their commandants could afford to be choosy, whilst both old and younger men often volunteered. Drawn, in the early days, from frontier farming stock, the Boer burgher was usually an excellent horseman, well used to living in the open in all conditions. Accustomed to hunting for provisions, he was a superb marksman.

The Boers fought in their every-day farming clothes, with no bright uniform to distinguish them from the natural colours of the veld, and excelled in field craft. They lacked the European professional soldiers' concept of do-or-die glory; for the Boer warfare was a necessary business, to be accomplished as effectively as possible, at minimum cost to one's self. Fighting was best done at long range with the rifle, and hand-to-hand combat was to be avoided, for death in battle carried too heavy a penalty for the burgher's family, left to fend for themselves on the veld. Highly mobile, the Boer commando traditionally lived off the land, and required little in the way of a baggage train. The Boer was, in short, the fore-runner of the hit-and-run guerrilla soldier of modern times.

Commandos were organised on the basis of peacetime administrative districts, and varied in size according to the level of the Afrikaner population; most, at the start of the Anglo-Boer War, averaged a thousand apiece, but figures as low as 200 and high as 3000 were not unknown. They were led by a *Commandant*, who was elected by the burghers under his command; he was supposed to be chosen for his military skill, but was often a man of some standing within the community. In civilian life, each district was broken down into wards administered by a *veld-kornet*, who served as a local magistrate, and in war-time the same men doubled as junior officers. A commando would therefore boast a commandant with several veld-kornets below him; in particularly large commandos, the veld-kornets might themselves have one or two assistants. The only other officers were corporals, who were elected as the representatives of informal

'Mournful Monday' – White's demoralised troops stream into Ladysmith after the defeats at Nicholson's Nek and Pepworth Hill on 30 October 1899.

'Mournful Monday' – British artillery withdrawing under heavy fire at the 'Battle of Ladysmith', 30 October, 1899.

groups of burghers who camped together. Although by 1899 the state could impose fines or even prison on any burgher who refused to join the commando, that was largely the extent of authority within the Boer ranks.

Neither commandants nor veld-kornets had any legal power to discipline their men, and most depended on the strength of their personality or reputations to ensure obedience. A commandant might issue orders, but he could not force his men to obey them; if they disagreed with them, the burghers were quite at liberty to ignore them. Nor could the burghers be prevented from taking leave whenever they chose; with farms and families at home to attend to, it was understood that periodic absences from the front were inevitable.

Although both sides tried to maintain the myth that the Anglo-Boer War was a 'White Man's War', both in fact made extensive use of black Africans. The Boers had no formal supply and commissariat departments, each man foraging for himself; as a result, many Boers took their black servants to the front with them. Known as *agterryers* ('after-riders'), their duty was to lead spare horse, drive wagons, and cook. Much of the drudgery of camp life fell to the black African, and as the war progressed, both sides used them increasingly as scouts, spies and, when the occasion demanded, did not scruple to include them in the front line.

Such was the raw material of the commando system; it had been tested in scores of small clashes against Africans across the length of South Africa, and even on occasion against the despised *roinek* – the sunburned British 'red-neck' Tommy. Yet by 1899 it had undergone some significant changes.

Both Republics had made an attempt to add a professional element to their forces. In 1880 the Free State had established the Free State Artillery, commanded by a German volunteer, Major Albrecht. In 1899 it consisted of over 20 assorted guns, and Albrecht, an efficient and conscientious officer, had ensured that it was well trained. The Transvaal, to whom the brunt of the quarrel with the British had fallen, had listened well to the warning of the Jameson Raid, and had been steadily arming since 1895. The Transvaal also had a regular artillery unit, the Staatsartillerie, which at the start of the war boasted 650 personnel, four heavy 150mm Creusot siege guns – which British intelligence reports mistakenly said could not be moved from their emplacements in the forts built around Pretoria – and about 50 other guns, mostly Creusot and Krupp 75mms, with a range of over 8000 yards, and 1-lb quick-firing Maxim-Nordenfeldt 'pom-poms'. The artillery of both Republics wore fine ceremonial uniforms based on Austrian and Dutch styles, but in the field these were replaced by drab fatigues where they wore uniforms at all. Neither did the Boers import the conventional European artillery concepts with their European guns. They did not deploy their artillery in batteries consisting of a number of guns in the open. Instead they used them singly, behind emplacements, moving them swiftly to command the best field of fire and avoid enemy detection. Both Republics also included trained Police units; the Transvaal ZARPs (*Zuid Afrikaanse Rijende Politie* – SA Mounted Police) despatched 400 men to the front in 1899. Their peacetime uniform consisted of a dark-blue tunic and cord riding breeches, and the ZARPs proved a determined force in battle. The Free State Police consisted of just 150 white men, and a number of black auxiliaries.

British infantry trudging through a rain-sodden landscape towards Ladysmith in the aftermath of the disasters of October 1899.

Two Boers on commando. Their dark civilian clothes and their weapons typify the appearance of the men who opposed Buller's advance on Ladysmith.

On the eve of the crisis, the Transvaal imported thousands of modern weapons. In the early 1890s, Joubert had ordered a large number British single-shot Martini-Henry rifles, but these were already obsolete, and at Kruger's insistence he switched to the 1896 model German 7mm Mauser. This was a highly efficient and accurate weapon, sighted to a maximum range of 2000 yards, with a magazine holding five rounds. These were loaded with a clip, which made the process simple and speedy. The Mauser used smokeless powder, which made it almost impossible to detect when fired by a concealed enemy, and often the distinctive double-crack of the shot was the only indication of an enemy's presence. These rifles were distributed amongst the commandos on the outbreak of war. Ammunition was carried in leather bandoliers which held 50 or 60 rounds.

In 1899 the Boer forces also included a number of small units made up of foreign volunteers. Not all of the *uitlanders* were of British descent, and there were a number who supported the Boer cause; these were sufficient to form 'corps' of Irish, American, Italian, German, Dutch and Scandinavian volunteers. Some of these – particularly the Germans and Scandinavians – included a number of former professional soldiers, who brought an incongruous touch of European-style discipline to the commandos. Some of these were issued clothing of a common pattern and colour – usually light khaki – and so had a rare degree of uniformity. Although the Boers themselves made no attempt at uniformity of dress, many were issued pressed brass badges in the form of the Transvaal or OFS coats-of-arms, which they wore on their hats, and coloured puggarees were fashionable in some commandos.

In the Transvaal Piet Joubert held the post of Commandant-General, an appointed office which lasted for five years. There was no Staff or Intelligence department to support him; he merely outranked the local commandants. However, the government did maintain the right to appoint *vecht commandants* (fighting generals), selecting them according to their abilities, and giving them command when a particular situation demanded it. Most command decisions were taken at a *krygsraad*, or council of war,

SOUTH AFRICA: THE BOER OFFENSIVES, OCT/NOV 1899

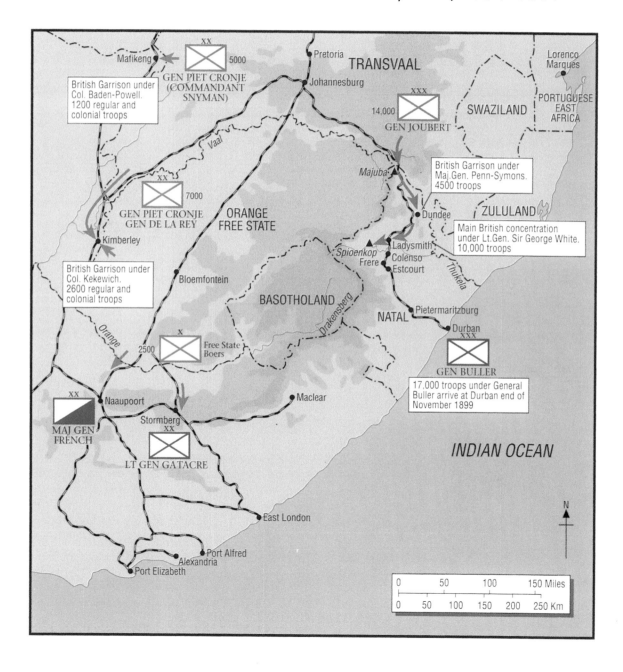

British Garrison under Col. Baden-Powell. 1200 regular and colonial troops

GEN PIET CRONJE (COMMANDANT SNYMAN)

5000

Mafikeng

Pretoria

TRANSVAAL

Lorenco Marques

Johannesburg

14,000 GEN JOUBERT

SWAZILAND

PORTUGUESE EAST AFRICA

Vaal

Majuba

British Garrison under Maj.Gen. Penn-Symons. 4500 troops

XX 7000

GEN PIET CRONJE GEN DE LA REY

ORANGE FREE STATE

Dundee

ZULULAND

Kimberley

Spioenkop Frere

Ladysmith Colenso Estcourt

Main British concentration under Lt.Gen. Sir George White. 10,000 troops

British Garrison under Col. Kekewich. 2600 regular and colonial troops

Bloemfontein

BASOTHOLAND

Drakensberg

NATAL

Pietermaritzburg

Durban XXX

Orange

X 2500

Free State Boers

Maclear

GEN BULLER

17,000 troops under General Buller arrive at Durban end of November 1899

XX MAJ GEN FRENCH

Naaupoort

Stormberg XX

LT GEN GATACRE

INDIAN OCEAN

East London

Port Alfred Alexandria Port Elizabeth

N

0   50   100   150 Miles
0   50   100   150   200   250 Km

The traditional top hat and
tails worn by the Boer
Commandant (top left) died out as the war became more severe and younger leaders emerged.
He is treating a member of the Staats Artillerie who wears the drab field uniform. This unit
greatly impressed the British with their professionalism and after their guns were lost later in the war they
reorganised as a mounted unit. The two figures in the foreground are typical of Boer volunteers. it was common,
particularly later in the war for worn out clothing to be replaced with captured British items. (Rick Scollins)

in which anyone had the right to speak; individuals could refuse to endorse the decision of the council, but if they gave it their support they were morally bound to follow its actions.

By 1899, the British were convinced that the Boers were a shadow of their former selves. There is, perhaps, some truth in this, and the image of the crack-shot Boer farmer as an invisible enemy has perhaps been over-stressed. By the outbreak of the war, a large proportion of the Afrikaner community lived in or around towns; some, as already noted, were *uit-landers*. Only a few in the ranks had any experience of actual warfare, and the days when most burghers lived by the game they hunted on their own farms were, like the game itself, long gone. Nor were they particularly used to handling their guns in action, since most were only issued with Mausers on the eve of war itself. Nevertheless, the commandos were required to undergo periodic shooting trials, when the burghers vied against each other to show off their shooting, and they were drawn from a culture which was individualistic, rugged, and accepted implicitly the ideal of the outdoor philosophy of the horse and the gun. In that they were infinitely more prepared for the coming conflict than their professional British coun-terpart.

A group of Boers typical in everything except armament; the man on the right holds an outdated single-shot Martini-Henry rifle, whilst three of the others are carry-ing British Lee-Metfords or Lee-Enfields. Such arms were imported by the Boer republics on the eve of the war, but were far outnum-bered by the German Mauser.

THE BRITISH

Commandant J H M Kock, centre, who commanded the Boer forces at Elandslaagte, and was killed there. He is surrounded by his staff, including a number of foreign volunteers and a Staatsartillerie officer (seated left) wearing his dress tunic.

By contrast, the British army in 1899 was very much a regular force. At the outbreak of war it boasted a total of 106,000 men with the Colours, and a further 78,000 men with the reserve. It was an army, furthermore, geared to the needs of policing an Empire at its zenith. Britain's Indian possessions alone required an enormous commitment, and thousands of men were stationed across the sub-continent at any given moment. Nor was it by any means a purely ceremonial army; during Queen Victoria's reign, there was scarcely a corner of the world in which it had not fought, from Ashante on the Gold Coast of Africa to China, and from Afghanistan to the South Island of New Zealand.

Yet the practical legacy of this combat experience was to prove confusing for the army in 1899. In some theatres, notably the trouble-some North-West Frontier, soldiers had been tested in a style of fighting which foreshadowed their experience in South Africa. Here, Afghan tribesmen had skirmished behind natural cover and sniped at their enemy at long-range, forcing their opponents to develop new theories of open-order rushes with fire support. Yet, on the whole, the military establishment had studied most the prevailing attitudes in European warfare, where parade-ground precision was still the order of the day. It was widely held that the most effective tactic was that of a protracted bombardment, followed by a close-order advance, with the troops pausing occasionally to deliver volley-fire. These formations were the easiest to teach the men, and they allowed the officers to exercise maximum control. Independent firing was frowned upon, not only because it lacked the moral effect of volley-fire, but also because it wasted ammunition.

Open-order formations were allowed for, as was the use of cover, but both were supposed to be subordinated to the need to maintain formation

ABOVE *This sketch of a skirmish outside Ladysmith suggests just how incompatible the tactics employed by the British were in the face of the excellent marksmanship and fieldcraft of the Boers.*

LEFT *A Boer 75mm Creusot. Such guns were the backbone of the Boer artillery, and the appearance of the gunners – a mixture of drab fatigues and civilian dress – is typical.*

and impetus. These tactics had served well in Britain's largest and most recent Colonial campaign, the reconquest of the Sudan. They made no provision, however, for the soldiers to act on their own initiative and did not develop individual marksmanship. The devastating effects of modern magazine fire had certainly been noted in the Sudan, where it had left white-clad Mahdist corpses piled up like snow-drifts in the desert, but the full implications of fighting a war in which both sides were armed with such weapons were not appreciated.

The characteristic which most epitomised the Boer volunteers was speed. It was this speed of movement which caught the British off balance during the early days of the war. Lightly equipped, carrying little other than food and ammunition, they proved an elusive enemy for the British regulars. (Michael Roffe)

Few British troops in 1899 believed anything other than that the Boer farmers of the Transvaal would quail before the steady line of bayonets advancing towards them, and in due course they would be proved horribly wrong. Despite its enormous superiority in manpower and military hardware, the mental rigidity and over-reliance on discipline which pervaded the British Army in 1899 made it singularly unsuited to the impending clash with a foe whose abiding characteristics were independence and agility of mind.

In 1881, the British Army had fought the Boers in the scarlet and blue of the Zulu War, almost the last major campaign in which they did so. By 1899, scarlet had long since given away to the sandy-colour known as khaki, and with khaki trousers and puttees, tunics and white foreign-service helmets with a khaki cover, there was little enough to distinguish the various arms of the service, let alone individual regiments. The uniform was made of light drill cloth, which had proved ideally suited to conditions in India, but was to prove too thin for the more varied climate of South Africa, and was later replaced with sturdier serge. The integrated Slade-Wallace equipment carried by the infantry, which allowed for 100 rounds to be carried in pouches either side of the belt buckle, was made of buff leather, but that too was usually dyed or muddied down in the field.

The only way units could distinguish one another were by coloured patches sewn onto the side of their helmet covers; most used a small patch of scarlet taken from their home service uniforms shoulder-straps, which had the name of their regiment embroidered in white. Some were more exotic; highland regiments usually adopted a piece of their regimental tartan, whilst the support services picked either their facing colour – deep crimson, for example, for the Royal Army Medical Corps – or, when several corps had the same facings, made an arbitrary choice, such as the Royal Engineers' canary yellow.

Naval 12-pdrs and their crews marching to relieve Ladysmith.

A lucky escape; the helmet worn by Lance Corporal C Mabey of the Somerset Light Infantry during the siege of Ladysmith, showing evidence of a near miss by a Boer bullet. The regimental flash – white badge and lettering on a red background – was typical of the distinctions adopted by British regiments early in the war. (Taunton Museum)

Troops embarking on an armoured train reconnaissance at Chieveley. Louis Botha successfully ambushed an expedition identical to this one on 15 November 1899.

Officers' rank was distinguished by shoulder pips; most wore brown Sam Browne belts and carried revolvers and swords. Although such differences made officers hard to distinguish from their men at a distance, even these made them too conspicuous to sharp-eyed Boers, and as the campaign progressed officers abandoned almost everything which marked their appearance different from that of their men, and fought with rifles.

British infantry carried bolt-action .303 magazine rifles, either the Lee-Metford or, steadily replacing it, the Lee-Enfield. These were sighted up to 2800 yards, but their effective battle range was between 500 and 800 yards. The magazines contained ten rounds, but these had to be loaded individually, which made the process slower than that of the Mauser, with its five-round clips. Infantry also carried knife-bladed bayonet whilst cavalry regiments were armed with a short Lee-Enfield carbine, swords and, for Lancer regiments, a nine-foot bamboo lance. Both infantry and cavalry regiments had two Maxim machine guns attached to them for support, but the full potential of these weapons was not fully appreciated, and they were not integrated into tactical thinking.

The backbone of the British regimental system was the infantry battalion – 800 men in companies of 100 men apiece. The old system of identifying line battalions by number had been abandoned in 1881, and battalions were now identified as part of a territorially-based regiment – for example, the old 58th Regiment, who had suffered heavily at Majuba, was now the 2nd Battalion, Northamptonshire Regiment. A cavalry regiment usually consisted of 600 men. Artillery batteries, both Royal Horse Artillery and Royal Field Artillery, consisted of six breach-loading guns, 12-pdrs for

These Privates from the 1st Royal Dragoons and 2nd Bn. Royal Irish Fusiliers are typical of the early part of the war before the bright regimental flashes were replaced with more subdued versions. The 1st Royal Dragoons were part of Dundonald's Mounted Brigade and the 2nd Bn., Royal Irish Fusiliers fought in Hart's Brigade at Colenso. (Pierre Turner)

Stuck in the mud – the realities of moving a British army across the South African veld are graphically illustrated by this photo of Buller's troops attempting to drag out a wagon stuck fast in a donga. (SB Bourquin)

the lighter Horse Artillery, and 15-pdrs for the field artillery. The 15-pdr could fire a shrapnel shell, which exploded with an air-burst, showering its target with lead balls, to a range of 4000 yards, and high explosive shell rather further, but it was still outranged by many of the guns possessed by the Boers. In 1899 artillery theorists were still committed to the concept of massed battery fire across open sights – communications systems had not yet developed to permit indirect fire – but despite this the guns possessed no shields to protect their crews from return fire.

The Army Corps assembled in Britain during the crisis of late 1899 consisted of 33 infantry battalions, a cavalry division of seven regiments, 19 batteries, including three of howitzers and four of horse artillery, with support corps, to a total of 47,000 men. Almost half of the men were reservists, who had to be recalled from civilian jobs to fill the ranks, and whilst the Corps was organised into Divisions and Brigades, few of these had any experience of serving together. The Corps was placed under the command of General Sir Redvers Buller, a long-standing member of Wolseley's clique, the 'Ashanti Ring', and one of the most highly regarded soldiers of his day. Buller took with him only his personal staff, however, since the Corps was singularly short on trained staff officers, many of whom had been sent out to South Africa in advance; circumstances would later deny Buller their use, and the Army Corps had to learn the lessons of working together in the painful school of active service. The Indian contingent, 10,000 strong, was commanded by Lieutenant-General Sir George White, a leading associate of Lord Roberts, Wolseley's chief rival. It did at least have some expe-

ABOVE *A 12-pdr Naval gun mounted on an improvised carriage; such guns were an invaluable addition to Buller's artillery in the Natal campaign.*

RIGHT *Brigadier-General Yule's troops reach Ladysmith after the gruelling retreat from Dundee, 26 October 1899.*

rience of working together, and the men were to some extent accustomed to the extreme conditions of life in the field.

Both White and Buller were light on cavalry, however. Indeed, few in the army establishment realised the extent to which cavalry would come to dominate a war fought over huge areas, some of which was still unmapped, and much of which lacked roads. To some extent they were able to rely on existing volunteer forces which had been raised in the colonies – notably the Cape Mounted Rifles at the Cape and Natal Carbineers and Mounted Police in Natal – and which were trained in a more military version of the Boers' fighting methods. These were augmented early in the war by several units raised from the *uitlander* refugees, notably Thorneycroft's Mounted Infantry, the South African Light Horse (and Infantry), and Bethune's Mounted Infantry. Although these units proved remarkably successful, they were far outnumbered by their Boer counterparts. Throughout most of the Anglo-Boer War the British army's pace of advance was limited to that of its infantry, and the huge train of baggage wagons it required to sustain itself in the field. Fighting a will-of-the-whisp enemy consisting almost entirely of mounted infantrymen, this was to prove a near-fatal handicap.

THE NATAL CAMPAIGN, OCT/NOV 1899

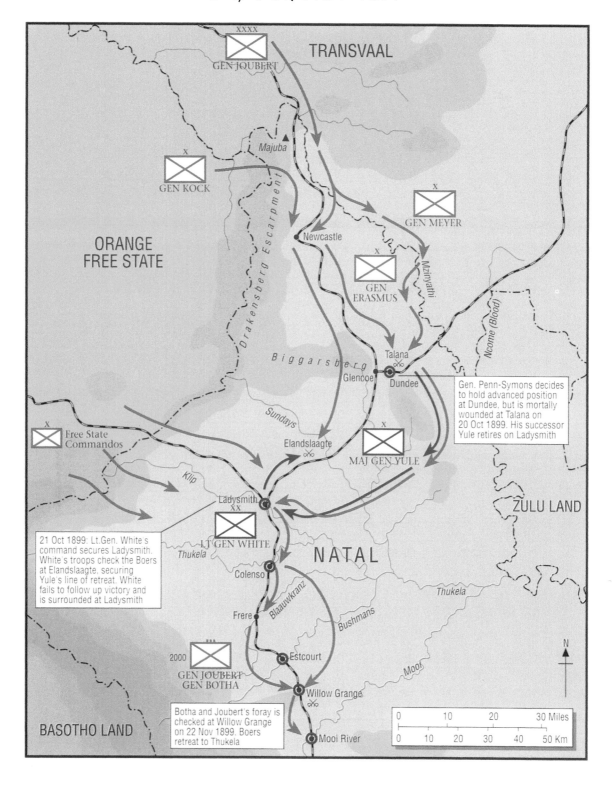

TRANSVAAL

XXXX
GEN JOUBERT

X
GEN KOCK

Majuba

X
GEN MEYER

ORANGE
FREE STATE

Drakensberg Escarpment

Newcastle

X
GEN
ERASMUS

Mzinyathi

Ncome (Blood)

Biggarsberg

Talana

Glencoe

Dundee

Gen. Penn-Symons decides
to hold advanced position
at Dundee, but is mortally
wounded at Talana on
20 Oct 1899. His successor
Yule retires on Ladysmith

X
Free State
Commandos

Sundays

Elandslaagte

X
MAJ GEN YULE

Klip

Ladysmith
XX

ZULU LAND

21 Oct 1899: Lt.Gen. White's
command secures Ladysmith.
White's troops check the Boers
at Elandslaagte, securing
Yule's line of retreat. White
fails to follow up victory and
is surrounded at Ladysmith

LT GEN WHITE

Thukela

NATAL

Colenso

Blaauwkranz

Thukela

Frere

Bushmans

2000
GEN JOUBERT
GEN BOTHA

Estcourt

Moor

Willow Grange

N

Botha and Joubert's foray is
checked at Willow Grange
on 22 Nov 1899. Boers
retreat to Thukela

BASOTHO LAND

Mooi River

0	10	20	30 Miles
0	10	20	30	40	50 Km

THE NATAL CAMPAIGN;
THE OPENING STAGES

W hite's troops arrived in Natal in October 1899, several weeks ahead of Buller's Army Corps. Opinions were divided in Natal as to the best way to defend the Colony, but White found that the local commander, Penn-Symons, had effectively made the decision for him. Natal was at its most vulnerable at its northern salient, where a triangle of land jutted out beneath the slope of the Drakensberg mountains. It was bordered to the west by the Free State and to the east by Zululand, whilst at the point it abutted the Transvaal. It was at this point that most of the fighting in the 1881 War had taken place, where Majuba mountain dominated the Laing's Nek pass through the Drakensberg. The salient boasted just two settlements of any significance, Newcastle in the north, and Dundee further south, and many argued that it made good sense to abandon these to the Boers, and to take up a defensive line further south, in the open country below the natural barrier of the Thukela river, which cut Natal in half.

There were, however, problems with this view. For one thing it galled the Natal administration to think that any of its inhabitants should be abandoned to the Boers, whilst the latent fear of a Zulu uprising argued against any military withdrawal from the borders. Furthermore, a retreat to the Thukela meant abandoning Ladysmith, the town just 18 miles north of it which had been the principle garrison town in Natal for several years. Buller, who had served in northern Natal during the Zulu War, had urged White not to go north of the Thukela; the country around Dundee was broken and rugged, and cut off from Ladysmith by a spur of the Drakensberg called the Biggarsberg. Whatever White's thoughts on the matter, however, he found by the time he arrived that Penn-Symons had moved 4500 men into the apex at Dundee itself. Penn-Symons was also a veteran of the Zulu War, a man who had a good deal of confidence in his own command, and very little respect for the Boers; he intended to stop the Boer invasion in its tracks as close to the border as possible. To support him, White advanced north of the Thukela to Ladysmith, and he had not long reached it when the first act of the Natal drama began.

The Boer advance into northern Natal was cautious, since Joubert expected to be opposed at any stage, and it proved difficult to control and co-ordinate the movements of the different commandos and their independent-minded commandants. However, Penn-Symons made little attempt to block Joubert's path. The Boers occupied Newcastle without a fight, and by 19 October they had advanced on Dundee. Before dawn on the 20th, Commandant Lukas Meyer took Penn-Symons by surprise when he occupied Talana Hill overlooking the town. Penn-Symons immediately drew his troops up in fine style and stormed the slopes of the hill, but the heavy casualties he suffered in the process were the first hint of the price to be paid when making frontal assaults in the face of heavy and accurate rifle-fire. Meyer abandoned Talana, but Penn-Symons' victory was tempered by the fact that he himself was mortally wounded during the fighting, and by the capture of much of his cavalry force, who had attempted a bold flanking march only to blunder right into the enemy under cover of a heavy mist. It soon became clear to Penn-Symons' successor, Major-General Yule, that the Boers still surrounded the town, and on White's advice Yule decided Dundee was indefensible. Leaving the dying Penn-Symons – and most of the townspeople – to the mercy of the Boers, Yule marched his force out of Dundee, and begun a gruelling retreat over the Biggarsberg towards White's garrison at Ladysmith, 45 miles away.

The news of Talana seemed to White to be encouraging when he first heard it. White knew that Joubert's Transvaal forces were advancing from the north in several distinct columns, whilst a further thrust was being made by the Free State commandos crossing the Drakensberg passes to the west. When his cavalry reported that the Free Staters had reached Elandslaagte station, cutting the railway line in Yule's rear, White determined to drive them out. Three infantry battalions, supported by cavalry and artillery, were sent out under the command of Major General Ian Hamilton, who, as a subaltern in the 92nd Regiment, had survived Majuba. The battle which followed on 21 October displayed the experience of the Indian contingent to good effect; in almost text-book style, they drove the Boers from one koppie to another, finishing off with a grim Lancer charge which caught the enemy in full retreat.

Nevertheless, Yule's retreat, and White's reluctance to follow his victory up, effectively neutralised the success at Elandslaagte. White contented himself with an inconclusive skirmish at Rietfontein three days later to prevent the Boers further threatening Yule's flank, and the next day Yule's men trudged into Ladysmith. Joubert, meanwhile, followed them up, and the Boers surrounded the town, taking possession of a number of flat-topped hills which rose from the plain in a ring around it. White remained largely unconcerned, however, and made plans for an audacious two-pronged night attack to break the cordon. In the darkness on 29/30 October he struck out at Boer positions on Pepworth Hill, east of the town, and at Nicholson's Nek, several miles away to the north. The subsequent actions, variously known as the Battle for Ladysmith, Nicholson's Nek, Pepworth or, simply, Mournful Monday, were a fiasco. The Pepworth contingent lost half its number in the dark, and dawn found it under severe flank attack from unsuspected Boer positions. On Nicholson's Nek the British practise of volley-firing proved so woefully inadequate in the face of aimed Boer fire that morale collapsed and most of the troops surrendered. When the army streamed back into Ladysmith, beaten, some of the on-lookers felt they were watching nothing less than a rout. For the first time White realised just how vulnerable his position in Ladysmith was; some 13,000 troops, their 2500 servants, and 5400 civilians were trapped within the confines of the little town of tin-roofed bungalows. Supplies were limited, and all were at the mercy of the Boer 150mm 'Long Toms', which were brought up to shell the town with impunity from the surrounding heights. Worse still, the Boers continued their advance, cutting the road and rail links to the south, and striking further into Natal.

THE PRELUDE TO COLENSO

In fact, with White bottled up at Ladysmith, a magnificent opportunity lay before the Boers. South of the town, the British line of communication followed the road and railway line which led to the provincial capital, Pietermaritzburg, and ultimately to Durban on the coast. This line was guarded by small garrisons which occupied the hamlets along the way — Chieveley, Frere and Estcourt. Yet there were scarcely any major concentrations of British troops between the Boers and Pietermaritzburg, or, indeed, the port of Durban itself. A determined advance on either might have undermined British resolve, and would have deprived them of the main harbour through which they intended to land their reinforcements.

Yet Joubert was a cautious man. The 68-year-old Commandant-General, who had been the senior Boer commander at Majuba in 1881, might have been known to his friends as 'Slim Piet' ('Clever Piet'), but he lacked the resolve to push forward with vigour, and hoped the investment of Ladysmith might in itself be enough to force the British to the negotiating table. Nor did he want to risk spreading his troops so thin; when pressed by his younger colleagues, he is supposed to have replied 'When God offers you his finger, don't try to take the whole hand'. Nevertheless, at the insistence of his younger second in command, Louis Botha, he allowed himself to be persuaded to make a tentative raid further south. Botha and Joubert took just 2000 men with them, but the whole of the Natal midlands lay open before them.

The garrison at the village of Colenso hastily fell back on a stronger force at Estcourt. Although the Boers were reluctant to attack Estcourt with White's troops in their rear, Botha's forces caught a British armoured train patrolling the track on 15 November. It was derailed by an obstruction on the line, and the trucks shot through with shells from a 75mm Creusot. Although the engine made good its escape, Botha captured a number of men, including a young journalist called Winston Churchill. By now, the first of Buller's Army Corps brigades had arrived in Natal, and, pushing on to the front, they tried to check Botha's progress at Willow Grange on the 22nd. It was in inconclusive fight, but enough to persuade Joubert to call off the foray and order a return to the Ladysmith lines.

General Buller had arrived at the Cape at the end of October, ahead of his Army Corps. In England, it had been decided that the best way to end the war would be to concentrate an attack on the western front, striking up first to Bloemfontein, the capital of the Free State, then on to Pretoria. This, it was argued, would cut the heart out of Boer resistance, and necessitate their withdrawal from Natal to face the threat. Although Buller himself supported this plan, the political realities on his arrival were such that he had to make an urgent move to support White in Natal. He could not, however, divert the entire Army Corps to Natal, since Cecil Rhodes, who had foolishly allowed himself to be caught up inside besieged Kimberley, was bellowing for assistance, whilst Milner, in turn, was worried about the security of the Cape. As a result, Buller decided to split the Corps; he would divert 16 infantry battalions, eight batteries and two cavalry regiments temporarily to Natal. Once Ladysmith had been relieved, the Corps would be concentrated once more for the advance on Bloemfontein. Although the Natal detachment was nominally under the command of Lieutenant-General Sir Francis Clery, Buller proposed to accompany it himself, and all the important decisions were to be his.

By the time Buller arrived in Natal, Botha had retreated north of the Thukela, but the situation was still not encouraging. Small parties of Boers were rampaging along the railway line, and a great number were deployed across the Thukela barrier, with White bottled up in Ladysmith beyond. White's supplies would not last forever, and since the Ladysmith force seemed paralysed by inertia, Buller had little choice but to try to dig them out. This would mean punching through the Boer line on the Thukela; the very barrier which the British themselves had regarded as formidable, and beyond which Buller had urged White not to go.

Buller was to receive much criticism for his handling of the subsequent campaign, but ironically he was one of the few who had a realistic idea of the difficulties which faced him. Immediately south of the Thukela the country was open and undulating, but beyond the river – a significant barrier itself, a hundred yards wide and swollen by early summer rain – the hills rose in a line of rocky terraces, scattered with boulders and bush, reaching a height of a thousand feet in some places above the plain.

Buller had served alongside the Boers in the Zulu War, and had learned to respect their fieldcraft; he realised that properly entrenched on the Thukela Heights, the Boers would be difficult to dislodge. Yet in truth there were little enough options, for the string of minor Boer successes made it politically imperative that Buller try to force a way through. The main route through to Ladysmith followed the railway line, which crossed the Thukela at the little town of Colenso, then wound through a maze of rocky hills before emerging into the open country beyond. Colenso offered a physical route – a road, the railway and bridges – but it was so obvious a point of attack that the Boers were sure to have entrenched it.

Buller concentrated his troops as they arrived at the hamlet of Frere, north of Estcourt. From here Buller contemplated the Boer lines, and his scouts searched for a way through. Fifteen miles upstream was another crossing point, Potgeiter's Drift, where a track also ran towards Ladysmith; here the hills opposite were higher, but in less depth. Buller's first plan was to move to his left and strike at Potgeiter's, hoping that the Boers might not have entrenched it as well as the more obvious Colenso route. On 10 December he ordered one of his infantry brigades, Barton's 6th (Fusiliers) Brigade, forward to Colenso to mask his imminent move to Potgeiter's. At that point, however, fate intervened.

Buller received information that fighting had taken place on the western front, and that it had gone badly. On 10 December Lieutenant-General Gatacre had mounted a daring night attack to deny the Boers the strategically important Stormberg railway junction in the Cape; the plan had miscarried in the darkness and Gatacre had lost 600 men killed or captured. On the Kimberley front just one day later, Lord Methuen had also advanced before dawn across an open plain to attack the Magersfontein heights; the Boers had opened fire from concealed trenches, and Methuen's attack collapsed in confusion, leaving over 200 dead on the field. Both battles had been deeply shocking to British pride; so far from running at the first sight of the bayonet, the Boers had in fact stopped the cream of the British army in its tracks. It was imperative that Buller made some headway in Natal to retrieve the situation; fearing that an attack on Potgeiter's might, after all, risk his lines of communication, and spurred on by the need for haste, Buller decided after all to attack by the obvious route. He would attack at Colenso.

THE COMMANDERS

General Sir Redvers Buller was 60 in 1899. He had distinguished himself under Sir Garnet Wolseley in West Africa in 1873, where the young, thrusting Wolseley had first gathered about him those officers who shared his revisionist views – the 'Ashanti Ring'. In Zululand in 1879 Buller had earned a VC in the debacle on Hlobane mountain, and had emerged with a fearsome reputation as a tough and indefatigable fighter. He had later fought in Egypt and the Sudan, but as he rose in rank Buller found himself increasingly desk-bound; when the Boer War broke out he was Commander at Aldershot. A big bulldog of a man with a famously gruff manner, Buller was loved by his men for the infinite pains he took to ensure their welfare; it was said that he never ate himself until his men had been fed. He seemed, in short, just the man to put 'Johnny Boer' in his place, and Press and public alike had cheered him off to war. Yet, as he grew older, Buller's touch had become less certain. He had commanded a Brigade in the Sudan with no great distinction, and he admitted himself that his showing on manoeuvres was sometimes poor. He had never commanded a force the size of the Army Corps in action before, and his private correspondence suggests that behind his fierce facade he was plagued by doubt. He knew how formidable the Boers could be. Furthermore, a taste for good living, cultivated at Aldershot, had perhaps slowed him down both physically and mentally. Yet the difficulties which faced Buller should not be under-estimated; in having to attack a defended position across open ground in the face of rapid rifle, Maxim and artillery fire, Buller was facing a tactical conundrum which would baffle a generation of officers on the Western Front in years to come. When an American attaché with Buller saw the Thukela line he asked simply, 'Isn't there any way round?' In truth there was not, not with the political consequences of delay hanging over his head, and it was Buller's tragedy that whilst he recognised the difficulty of the position, most of those around him had supreme confidence in his ability to overcome it.

Buller's commanders all had similarly impressive experience to their credit, though it had prepared few enough of them for the task at hand. Lieutenant-General Sir Francis Clery had served on Lord Chelmsford's staff in the Zulu War; a former professor of tactics at Sandhurst, he had been scathing of his fellow officers in that campaign, but 20 years on found him

General Redvers Buller, who commanded British forces during the relief of Ladysmith. Buller was a national hero, for whom the Boer war brought disgrace, yet the tactical problems which he faced were undoubtedly severe.

Major-General A Fitzroy 'No-Bobs' Hart, who commanded the Irish Brigade during the Natal campaign.

Major-General Neville Lyttleton, who commanded the 4th Brigade at Colenso.

vain and cautious. Clery dyed his greying whiskers blue, and refused to act without Buller's approval; indeed, Buller's presence effectively robbed him of an independent command.

Of the infantry brigade commanders, perhaps the most imaginative and decisive of them was Major-General Neville Lyttleton, commanding the 4th (Light) Brigade, who had served in India and had commanded a brigade at Omdurman, only a year before, in the climactic battle of the Sudanese reconquest. Major-General Henry Hildyard, 2nd Brigade, had fought at Tel-El-Kebir in Egypt in 1882, and had recently commanded at the Staff College, a position which seems to have impressed on him the importance of handling troops properly in action. Both of the remaining infantry Brigade commanders were veterans of the Zulu War; Major-General Geoffrey Barton, commanding the 6th (Fusiliers) Brigade, had also seen action in Egypt and the Sudan, but was to prove an unadventurous and cautious leader in South Africa. Steely-eyed Major-General Alan Fitzroy Hart, commanding the 5th (Irish) Brigade, was known to his men as 'No-Bobs Hart' from his undoubted personal courage and his disdain of ducking when under fire. He was a firm believer in 'keeping the men in hand' by maintaining close order in battle, and in the moral effect of the bayonet charge.

Buller's senior artillery man, Colonel Charles Long, who had commanded the garrison at Estcourt, was also a believer in close-order fighting; at the battle of the Atbara in the Sudan in 1898 he galloped his batteries up close to the Mahdist camp, and unleashed such a fury of fire that according to one eyewitness it looked afterwards as if it had been rolled flat by

Major-General H J T Hildyard, commanding the 2nd Brigade; Hildyard's attack on Colenso village was one of the few successful manoeuvres during the battle.

RIGHT *Major-General Geoffrey Barton whose 6th Brigade remained steadfastly in reserve at Colenso.*

ABOVE RIGHT *Colonel Charles Long, whose two batteries suffered so heavily at Colenso; Long was seriously wounded in the action, but survived.*

a steamroller. Commanding the Cavalry Division was Colonel Lord Dundonald, the embodiment of the dashing cavalry tradition, an original thinker, if a little eccentric.

Among the Boers facing Buller across the river, there had been an ominous change of command on the eve of battle. During the raid into Natal, Commandant-General Joubert had fallen from his horse, and the accident robbed him of his taste for war. Joubert took the train back to Pretoria to recover, and his absence allowed the young and thrusting Louis Botha to move to the fore. Botha was just 37 at the start of the Anglo-Boer War, much younger than most of his fellow commandants in a system which equated age with authority; he had been born near Greytown, in Natal, to a family with good Voortrekker credentials, but he had grown up in the Free State, and in 1884 had joined Lukas Meyer's commando which had fought in the Zulu civil war. It was Botha's first taste of warfare, and it earned him a farm near Vryheid, just across the border from Natal. Later, when Vryheid became absorbed into the Transvaal, Botha had represented his district on the Transvaal Volksraad.

Botha's upbringing mitigated against the parochialism which characterised so many of his fellow commandants, and, although Botha had close political ties with both Joubert and Meyer, it was his instinctive military capacity which assured his rapid rise to a position of high command. When Penn-Symons chased Meyer's Vryheid commando off Talana, Meyer had retired from the war, leaving Botha in command of the Vryheid men. Soon Botha was appointed a special *vecht commandant*, fighting general, and he left his mark on Joubert's raid into Natal. When Joubert took leave, Botha

General Louis Botha is cheered through the streets by supporters during a return from the Natal front in May 1900. (National Army Museum)

Colonel Lord Dundonald who commanded the Cavalry Brigade throughout the Natal campaign.

General Louis Botha, the Boer hero of the Natal campaign. (National Army Museum)

assumed over-all command of the Thukela sector. Where Joubert was old and cautious, Botha was confidant and daring; he knew his people well, when to cajole, when to bully, and when to threaten them with the wrath of the Lord and Paul Kruger. His tent was open to any back-veld farmer who had a grievance to share, and when an elderly man entered it, Botha gave up his chair and squatted on the floor. As a result, he was able to galvanise the Boers like few of his contemporaries.

Nevertheless, there were limits to Botha's capacity to resist. Although Buller in his gloomier moments guessed that the Boers had deployed 50,000 men on the Thukela line, there were only 14,000 in the Natal theatre, and half in fact remained in the laagers around Ladysmith. Botha had no more than 7000 to guard a line which stretched potentially from the Drakensberg mountains to the hills east of Colenso – a distance of over 50 miles. He had little choice but to screen the most obvious points of attack, and to patrol the sectors in between, trusting to the slowness of the British advance to give him ample time to concentrate his forces. Colenso was an obvious choice; in the event, Buller did not disappoint him.

THE BATTLE OF COLENSO

The Thukela winds in great loops below the heights near Colenso. The village itself, a scattering of tin roofed bungalows and a railway station, nestled in one such loop, commanding two bridges across the river. The most impressive of these, an iron trestle railway bridge, Botha had destroyed during his raid towards Estcourt, so as to deny it to the British. Immediately to the left of Colenso, however, a little way upstream, another bridge, used to convey wagon traffic across the river, had been left intact. This was a deliberate ploy on Botha's part.

There was nothing particularly sophisticated in the concept of Botha's defensive plan, but its virtue lay in the skill with which it was carried out. South of the river – on the British side – the terrain sloped gently down to the Thukela, with little enough cover to obscure the British movements. On the Boer side, however, there was a basin of undulating country immediately north of Colenso itself, broken here and there by several rocky outcrops – the Colenso Koppies. One of these, which local Colonial troops had fortified earlier in the campaign, was known as Fort Wylie, and commanded the demolished railway bridge. North of the Colenso Koppies, however, the land rose up in several terraces to a line of steep hills, slashed

A Boer 75mm Creusot on the heights overlooking the Thukela. The strength of Botha's position is clearly shown by this photograph; Colenso village is visible in the left background, whilst on the right is the Thukela loop, where Hart's brigade came to grief. (National Army Museum)

British troops bivouacking on the north bank of the Thukela before the assault on the Boer positions on Hart's, Railway and Pieter's Hills on the skyline. (National Army Museum)

through here and there with steep gorges. Botha made no attempt to defend the river, but hoped simply to use it as a barrier to concentrate the British force; indeed, he hoped the surviving bridge might serve to funnel them into the open spaces below the Colenso Koppies. Here, with a point of retreat so narrow as to be impractical under fire, he intended to cut them off, and destroy them with his artillery, which was placed piecemeal on the heights. He had just 4500 men available on the Colenso sector, and these he deployed in a broken line between the foot of the hills and the river.

The Free State men, the Johannesburg and Middleburg commandos, he placed upstream of Colenso, in case the British tried to cross at a ford known as Robinson's Drift. The Ermelo, Zoutpansberg and Swaziland commandos were deployed along the edge of a great loop of the river between Robinson's Drift and Colenso. The Boksburg, Heidelberg, Vryheid and Krugersdorp commandos, with the Johannesburg ZARPs, held the Colenso Koppies and Fort Wylie, whilst the Wakkerstroom and Standerton commandos secured Hlangwane hill on Botha's extreme left. The Boers were protected here and there by natural cover or existing stone walls, and they linked the rest of the line with carefully concealed trenches. Here they remained largely hidden until the battle proper began.

Not that the Boer position was invulnerable, and, indeed, the left had already given Botha cause for concern. Just downstream from Colenso, the Thukela turns sharply north, leaving the Hlangwane ridge isolated on the southern bank. Since the latter effectively commands the flank of Fort Wylie and the Colenso Koppies, any British force which could capture it would be able to enfilade a crucial part of Botha's line. It was therefore crucial that Hlangwane be held, but the Boers showed a distinct reluctance to occupy this dubious post of honour, since the river behind them effectively cut off their retreat. The men originally stationed there had abandoned their post in the face of the obvious British preparations for attack,

and it took all of Botha's powers, backed up by a telegram from Kruger himself, to cajole and bully the Boers back into line. The Wakkerstroom and Standerton men only agreed to re-occupy the hill on the night of 14 December – the day before the battle.

To attack the Colenso position, Buller had four infantry brigades (each of four battalions), a cavalry division, five batteries of artillery, and assorted Naval guns. These were heavy ships' guns landed at Durban from four Royal Navy ships, mounted on improvised carriages, and dragged up from Durban by oxen; the largest of them, 4.7 in. guns, had a range of 10,000 yards, and they were a significant addition to Buller's arsenal.

Barton's Brigade was already in position between Chieveley and Colenso, and in the second week of December cavalry patrols were pushed out to the river itself in an attempt to feel out the Boer positions, but Botha kept his men well in hand, and they gave the British no clues of their whereabouts or numbers. The 4.7 in. guns were advanced to a rise near Barton's camp, and began to shell the heights 5000 yards away on the 13th, again to no obvious effect. By the evening of 14 December, Buller had concentrated his forces nearby, and laid his plans for a dawn attack the following morning.

Buller's plan was simple; it took little account of his own view that the Colenso position was too strong to be taken by direct assault, although Buller's lack of confidence soon became apparent in the hesitant way the

The heights opposite the Thukela, from the British position in January 1900. The point marked E is the Ntabamnyama plateau; A is the summit of Spioenkop. B is Aloe Knoll, and C and D mark the approximate positions of Schalk Burger's guns. (King's Own Museum, Lancaster)

FIRST ATTEMPTS TO RELIEVE LADYSMITH:
COLENSO & SPIOENKOP

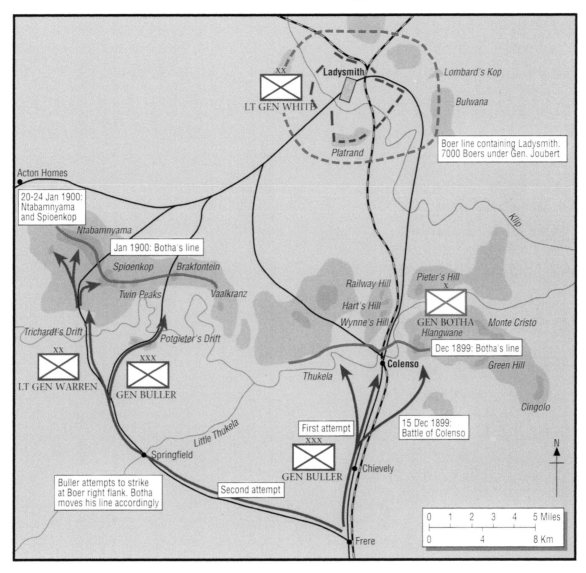

attack was handled. Buller needed to force a way across the river; the intact road bridge was all too obviously a trap, but according to his inaccurate and incomplete maps, there was at least one good drift upstream of the loop in the river to the west of the village. If Buller knew of Robinson's Drift, further upstream, he took no account of it. Instead, he intended to launch one brigade – Hildyard's 2nd – against Colenso itself, whilst another – Hart's – would strike at the drift to the right. Both brigades would be supported by artillery, whilst the two remaining brigades (Lyttleton's and Barton's) would remain in support. The heavy Naval guns would shell the heights from a rise in the rear. Privately, Buller later admitted that he had

The ruined railway bridge across the Thukela at Colenso, with the koppie known as Fort Wylie behind. This photograph was taken later in the war when a temporary bridge had been rebuilt.

Lieutenant Ogilvy's Navy 12-pdrs advancing to the front at Colenso. This illustration clearly shows the flat ground occupied by the British, with the Boer-held heights beyond. The smoke from Long's guns can be seen in the middle-distance on the right.

no very clear idea how he would proceed if he secured a crossing, and he dreaded fighting in the gorges further north along the railway-line. Although Buller was in touch with White's forces in Ladysmith by heliograph, he was convinced that the Colenso position was too far away for White to make any diversionary attack to support him, and so did not demand it.

It is a curious feature of this plan that it failed to take account of the vulnerability of the Boer line from Hlangwane. Buller was apparently reluctant to risk his troops in this, their first taste of South African warfare, over broken terrain which would inevitably have disrupted their formations, and he may well have over-estimated the strength of the Boer forces on the ridge. It is also conceivable, however, that he failed to appreciate the extent to which Hlangwane dominated the Colenso Koppies, since the

RIGHT No 5 gun, 14th Battery, under fire at Colenso. Although this picture stresses the exposed nature of Long's command, his casualties were sustainable, and it was problems with ammunition supply that eventually made his position untenable.

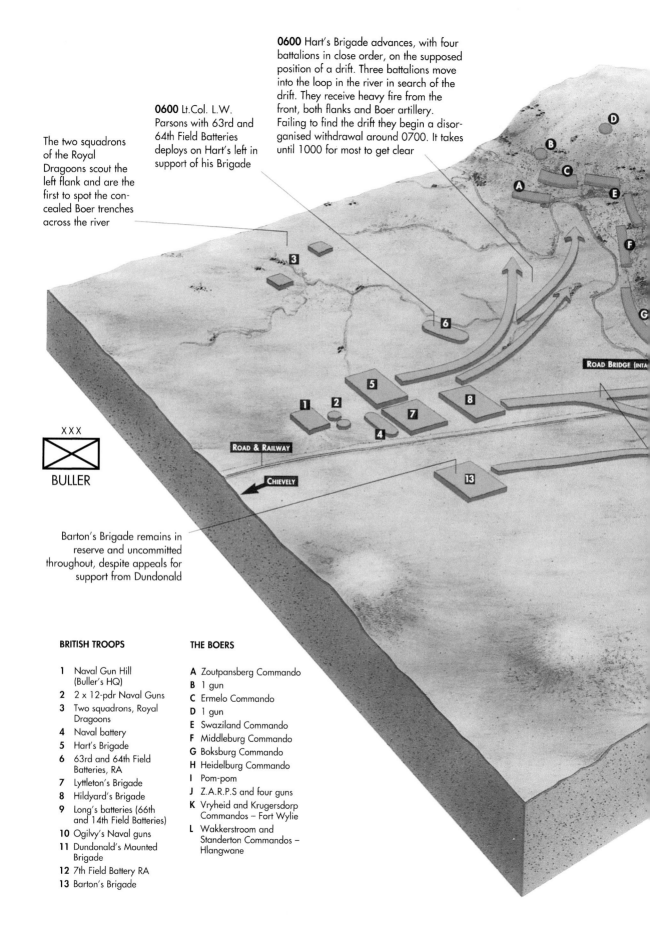

0600 Hart's Brigade advances, with four battalions in close order, on the supposed position of a drift. Three battalions move into the loop in the river in search of the drift. They receive heavy fire from the front, both flanks and Boer artillery. Failing to find the drift they begin a disorganised withdrawal around 0700. It takes until 1000 for most to get clear

0600 Lt.Col. L.W. Parsons with 63rd and 64th Field Batteries deploys on Hart's left in support of his Brigade

The two squadrons of the Royal Dragoons scout the left flank and are the first to spot the concealed Boer trenches across the river

XXX

BULLER

Barton's Brigade remains in reserve and uncommitted throughout, despite appeals for support from Dundonald

ROAD & RAILWAY

← CHIEVELY

ROAD BRIDGE [INTA

BRITISH TROOPS

1 Naval Gun Hill (Buller's HQ)
2 2 x 12-pdr Naval Guns
3 Two squadrons, Royal Dragoons
4 Naval battery
5 Hart's Brigade
6 63rd and 64th Field Batteries, RA
7 Lyttleton's Brigade
8 Hildyard's Brigade
9 Long's batteries (66th and 14th Field Batteries)
10 Ogilvy's Naval guns
11 Dundonald's Mounted Brigade
12 7th Field Battery RA
13 Barton's Brigade

THE BOERS

A Zoutpansberg Commando
B 1 gun
C Ermelo Commando
D 1 gun
E Swaziland Commando
F Middleburg Commando
G Boksburg Commando
H Heidelburg Commando
I Pom-pom
J Z.A.R.P.S and four guns
K Vryheid and Krugersdorp Commandos – Fort Wylie
L Wakkerstroom and Standerton Commandos – Hlangwane

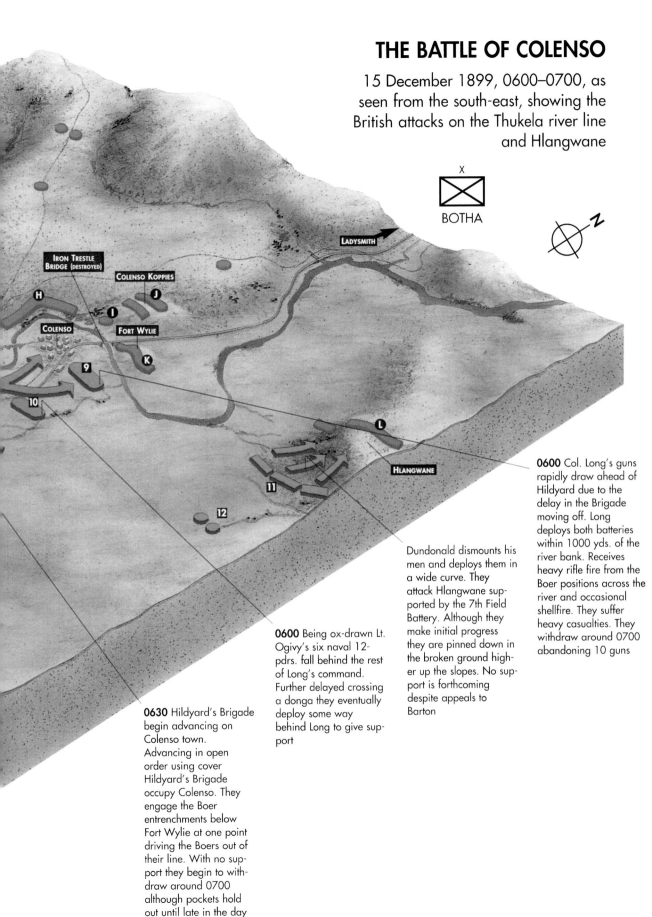

THE BATTLE OF COLENSO

15 December 1899, 0600–0700, as seen from the south-east, showing the British attacks on the Thukela river line and Hlangwane

BOTHA

IRON TRESTLE BRIDGE (DESTROYED)

COLENSO KOPPIES

LADYSMITH

COLENSO

FORT WYLIE

HLANGWANE

H

J

I

K

9

10

11

12

L

0600 Col. Long's guns rapidly draw ahead of Hildyard due to the delay in the Brigade moving off. Long deploys both batteries within 1000 yds. of the river bank. Receives heavy rifle fire from the Boer positions across the river and occasional shellfire. They suffer heavy casualties. They withdraw around 0700 abandoning 10 guns

Dundonald dismounts his men and deploys them in a wide curve. They attack Hlangwane supported by the 7th Field Battery. Although they make initial progress they are pinned down in the broken ground higher up the slopes. No support is forthcoming despite appeals to Barton

0600 Being ox-drawn Lt. Ogivy's six naval 12-pdrs. fall behind the rest of Long's command. Further delayed crossing a donga they eventually deploy some way behind Long to give support

0630 Hildyard's Brigade begin advancing on Colenso town. Advancing in open order using cover Hildyard's Brigade occupy Colenso. They engage the Boer entrenchments below Fort Wylie at one point driving the Boers out of their line. With no support they begin to withdraw around 0700 although pockets hold out until late in the day

course of the river was obscured by bush and trees, and it may even be that Buller supposed the Thukela ran in front of Hlangwane. In any case, Lord Dundonald's cavalry, supported by a single battery of artillery, was given the job of attacking Hlangwane, but this was intended merely to secure the British right flank. Hlangwane was not seen as a significant objective in its own right.

The attack began before dawn on the 15th. Hildyard's, Lyttleton's and Hart's Brigades had been assembled to the left of the railway line, opposite Barton's, and as the long lines of infantry advanced they threw up a cloud of dust which hung at waist height in the still morning air. The plan began to go awry almost from the start. Hildyard's brigade was slow in moving off, and its supporting artillery, commanded by Colonel Long, soon drew ahead. Buller later claimed that he had been most specific in ordering Long to deploy at a particular spot on the map, well away from the river, but the maps were unreliable, and as Long's guns crossed to the right of the railway track they were soon abreast of Colenso itself. Perhaps Long, in any case, was keen to follow the tactics which had earned him such laurels at Atbara; perhaps he simply thought the Boer positions were further off. For whatever reason Long deployed his two batteries of field artillery – the 66th and 14th – less than a thousand yards from the river bank.

He also commanded six naval 12-pdrs under Lieutenant Ogilvy, but these, being ox-drawn, had fallen behind, and were further delayed crossing a deep donga several hundred yards in Long's rear. When Long's gunners deployed with parade-ground precision and fired their first salvo, guessing at the location of their targets, they were therefore entirely unsupported.

'A Devil of a mess'. The leading companies of Hart's brigade, pinned down and under fire, trapped in the Thukela loop at the battle of Colenso.

BRITISH

Commander
GENERAL SIR REDVERS BULLER

Hildyard's 2nd (English) Brigade
2nd Royal West Surrey
2nd West Yorkshire
2nd East Surrey
2nd Devonshire

Lyttleton's 4th (Light) Brigade
2nd Scottish Rifles
1st Durham Light Infantry
1st Rifle Brigade
3rd King's Royal Rifle Corps

Colonel Long
14th and 66th Field Batteries
Lieutenant Ogilvy
6 x 12-pdr Naval guns

Barton's 6th (Fusilier) Brigade
1st Royal Welsh Fusiliers
2nd Royal Irish Fusiliers
2nd Royal Scots Fusiliers
2nd Royal Fusiliers

Hart's 5th (Irish) Brigade
1st Connaught Rangers
2nd Royal Dublin Fusiliers
1st Royal Inniskillin Fusiliers
1st Scottish Borderers

Colonel Parsons
63rd and 64th Field Batteries

Dundonald's Mounted Brigade
1st Royal Dragoons
13th Hussars
Composite Regiment, Mounted Infantry
Bethune's Mounted Infantry
Thorneycroft's Mounted Infantry
South African Light Horse
7th Field Battery

Unattached
2 x 4.7 in. guns
6 x 12-pdr. Naval guns

THE BOERS

Commander
COMMANDANT LOUIS BOTHA

The Zoutpansberg, Middleburg,
Swaziland, Ermelo, Standerton,
Boksburg, Heidelburg, Johannesburg
Police, Vryheid, Krugersdorp,
Standerton and Wakkerstroom
Commandos.

1 x 5-in. Krupp Howitzer
10 x 75mm Creusot and Krupp Guns
1 x Maxim-Nordenfeldt pom-pom

The words of command echoed eerily across the veld as Long began firing. From a position on the opposite heights, Botha gave the signal to reply; a single shot from a howitzer. Immediately the Boer marksmen concealed in their trenches below Fort Wylie opened fire. A storm of Mauser fire, supported by occasional shells from the heights above, broke over Long's men. A thousand yards was long range for small arms, even for the Boers, and the fire was not particularly accurate, but the air around the batteries hummed with bullets. The men stuck to their duties with admirable coolness, but the officers particularly attracted fire. Two of Long's battery commanders were killed, and Long himself was seriously wounded through the liver by a shrapnel ball, and carried to the rear.

To the left, Hart's brigade had by now become engaged, and was also in difficulties. Hart had pressed forward towards the river in fine style, true to his reputation; his battalions were lined up in close-order, the Dublin Fusiliers in front with the Inniskillins behind, and the Border Regiment and Connaught Rangers in support. Lieutenant-Colonel L W Parsons, supporting Hart with the 63rd and 64th Field Batteries, deployed

on Hart's left – though he received no instructions from Hart on how best to use them – whilst beyond him detachments of the 1st Royal Dragoons scouted the flank. There was still no sign of the Boers, but the cavalry were the first to spot them, concealed in trenches just across the river, threatening Hart's flank. Their commander sent a message to Hart warning him of the danger, but Hart, still placing his faith in the close-order attack, replied that he intended to take no notice of the enemy unless they interfered with his movements.

Officers watching the progress of the battle of Colenso from Buller's headquarters on Naval Gun Hill in the rear; note the Naval 12-pdr, centre.

As he reached the river, however, Hart's position became confused. He was looking for a drift to the left of the loop in the river, marked on the maps as the Bridle Drift, but somehow the dongas he had crossed did not seem to be where they should have been, and the direction of his advance was not at all clear. He had an African guide with him, who insisted that the only viable drift lay further to the right. This was dangerous news, since to Hart's right front lay the loop in the Thukela. Given the news that the Boers were on the far side of the loop in numbers, and advance in that direction was fraught with difficulties, to enter the loop would expose Hart's Brigade to enfilading as well as frontal fire. Hart, however, was made of stern stuff, and did not falter.

Leaving the Border Regiment at the river, he led his remaining three battalions into the loop. He had not gone far when a storm of Mauser fire swept down on him, devastating the front ranks and lashing his flanks. Several companies tried to shake themselves into open order, but Hart, who was possessed of not only tremendous personal courage but also a charmed

life, insisted that they close up. The vanguard of the Dublin Fusiliers pushed almost into the apex of the loop itself, where an African homestead provided some cover, and a handful of men reached the banks and searched for a way across. Any drift that might have been there was submerged in the summer flow, however, and most of these men were either shot or drowned. The remainder lay down on the open grassland, as the Creusot guns concealed on the slopes of Grobbelaar's Kop added their quota to the firestorm.

Buller, back on the rise christened Naval Gun Hill, seemed surprised by the turn of events. For all the fire they were laying down, neither the Boer guns nor their trenches could be at all clearly distinguished, because of the smokeless powder they were firing. Though the Naval guns continued to shell the distant heights, there was little enough for them to fire at. So far only two of his four brigades had been committed, but Buller was angry that Long had so exposed himself. Initial reports suggested that Long was holding his own, but when the maelstrom broke over Hart, Buller quickly rode forward to try to sort out what already seemed to him to be 'a devil of a mess'.

Buller first encountered Hildyard's brigade, which was still moving up towards Colenso — it was still no later than 0630, just half an hour after the first shots had been fired. He ordered them to press forward their attack, to try to relieve the pressure on Long, and rode over to see for himself what had become of the guns. Despite their position, the batteries appeared to be doing well; their casualties were mounting, but they had fired off all of the ammunition in their limbers, and had succeeded in suppressing the fire of at least one Boer gun in front of them.

More ammunition had been fetched from the rear, and Ogilvy's guns had now deployed some way behind them to offer them some support. Nevertheless, a crisis quickly developed as the second supply of ammunition was expended. More was sent for, but the reserve was a long way down the track, and after almost an hour of continuous firing, Long's guns fell quiet. There was little point in the gunners staying there to be shot at,

so they ran back to the cover of a small donga to the rear. Here Buller found them, and he directed the rest of the battle from this quite inappropriate spot.

The attempt to save the guns; Lieutenant Freddy Roberts falls mortally wounded, right.

Aware, now, of just how bad Hart's position had become, Buller ordered Lyttleton's brigade forward to support it. Lyttleton moved towards the river, but came under heavy fire before he reached it He deployed his men in open order, giving what covering fire they could. Some of Hart's companies had realised the hopelessness of their position and were already moving away from the loop, but many were reluctant to do so. For most, indeed, retreat exposed them to the Mausers as much as the advance had done, and the men simply lay down under the fire and did not move. Here and there Hart had been able to encourage a few to advance, but with no clear objective, this had become pointless. When the order finally went out to abandon the attack, some isolated pockets never received it. The withdrawal, inevitably, was a disorganised affair.

On the right, Dundonald's attack on Hlangwane had also stalled. Dundonald had dismounted his men and deployed them in a wide curve, the South African Light Horse on the left, the Composite Regiment – an amalgam of the various mounted units at Estcourt, in the centre, and Thorneycroft's Mounted Infantry on the right, with the 7th Field Battery supporting in the rear. Although Dundonald's men had scrambled up the lower slopes of Hlangwane in style, they had been met by a heavy Boer

fire from the summit, and the attacks had, as Buller had feared, become bogged down in the maze of boulder-strewn folds and gullies. Without considerable reinforcement, there was little more Dundonald could do, and he called on Barton's infantry brigade for support. So far Barton had hung back and was entirely uncommitted, but he would not advance without Buller's order, and Buller, already sensing that the attack was failing, would not order Barton to move.

Buller, meanwhile, was addressing the problem of Long's guns. The guns now stood in the open, surrounded by dead and wounded gunners, and Boer fire played on them at will. Indeed, Buller himself had had a close shave from shrapnel fire; his personal physician was killed, and Buller had been struck in the side by a spent ball, an injury he concealed from those around him. Several limbers from the two batteries were near the donga, under cover, and Buller ordered one of his ADC's, Captain Schofield, to try to recover some of the guns. With a handful of volunteers, Schofield rushed forward with the limbers and managed to drag away two guns.

This movement was so bold that it seems to have caught the Boers by surprise, but when a second attempt was made the Boers were waiting. This attempt was led by Lieutenant Freddy Roberts, the son of Buller's 'India Ring' rival, Lord Frederick Roberts. Drivers and horses were shot down alike, and the attempt had to be abandoned; among those hit was Freddy Roberts, who was carried to the rear, shot through the body and mortally wounded.

Only in the centre were the British having any luck. Hildyard's Brigade, deployed in open order and advancing carefully, making good use of any cover, had occupied Colenso. They deployed among the buildings and behind garden walls and fences, opening fire on the Boer trenches they could now see below Fort Wylie. At one point the Boers were driven out of their line, but when an order was sent for artillery support, it was cancelled in the belief that the running figures were in fact advancing British troops. There was little, indeed, that Hildyard could do on his own, and at about 0700 Buller called off the attack.

Retiring was not an easy task. Hart's men limped away from the river, whilst Lyttleton covered them until most were out of range. It was after

A dramatic sketch of the end of the day at Colenso; exultant Boers cross the river to take possession of Long's guns, abandoned on the skyline, left.

1000 before most of them were clear, and here and there a few pockets held their ground throughout the day, unaware of the general retreat. When a party of Boers cautiously crossed the river to examine the battlefield in the afternoon, the subsequent encounter took both sides by surprise. The British troops refused to surrender, and rather than risk a fresh outbreak of fighting the Boers let them retire. Much the same thing happened in Colenso itself, where a party of the 2nd Devons held out in the town until late in the day. Here, too, the Boers crossed over, lured by the sight of Long's abandoned guns, and the Devons were surrounded. In an exchange between the two sides, the Devons' commanding officer refused to surrender, but a Boer knocked him down with his rifle-butt, and his men were quickly rounded up.

Most galling of all, however, was the loss of the guns of the 14th and 66th Batteries. The gunners had left them expecting shortly to return, and had made no attempt to disable them. Now, at Buller's insistence, they retired from the field, leaving the ten remaining guns abandoned in the open. It might have been possible to cover their position and return after dark to collect them, but after the carnage wrought on Freddy Roberts' party, Buller seems to have lost heart. Later that same day, a party of jubilant Boers dragged the guns away unmolested.

The attack at Colenso had lasted scarcely an hour. It was not, in truth, a disaster; Buller's advance had been checked, but he had called it off before his position had become serious. Nor had he conceded ground to his enemy by the withdrawal, since Botha did not venture out of his secure position to cross the Thukela. At least one of Buller's Brigades had not been engaged at all, whilst the British casualties amounted to seven officers and 138 men killed, 43 officers and 719 men wounded, and 21 officers and 199 men missing or captured. Of these, over 500 casualties had been in Hart's Brigade, whilst Long's two batteries had lost two officers and seven men killed, and six officers and 20 men wounded, with a further five officers and 44 men missing.

Many of those wounded were not seriously hurt, and the majority were back in the ranks within weeks. These were not the sort of casualties to immobilise an Army of 18,000 men; indeed, the most serious loss was undoubtedly Long's guns themselves, which made up nearly a third of Buller's available artillery, and almost doubled that now available to Botha. Six VCs were awarded for the action; both Captain Schofield and Freddy Roberts were among them, but the latter died before he received his.

Botha's losses were negligible – perhaps 40 men killed and wounded altogether. The Boer commander had needed no great tactical genius to win the day; Buller had simply come knocking on his front door, and Botha had refused him entry. Nevertheless, whilst Buller bitterly complained that Long had spoilt his entire plan – 'sold by a damned gunner!' was his gruff comment to an ADC – Botha realised that Long's actions had spared the British a worse fate. By provoking a Boer response earlier than Botha had anticipated, Long's batteries had destroyed any chance of a British foray across the remaining bridge, with all the greater slaughter that must inevitably have entailed.

THE AFTERMATH OF COLENSO

Militarily, the defeat at Colenso hardly affected the British position, but, coming so soon upon the defeats at Magersfontein and Stormberg, it assumed the proportions of a national calamity. It was hailed across the Empire as the culmination of 'Black Week', provoking a jingoistic howl of protest from the British politicians, Press and public alike, and inspiring the Colonies to offer to send troops to the mother country's relief.

The battle had confirmed Buller's inner doubts. He had felt the Colenso position was a 'forlorn hope', and so it had proved; outwardly Buller blustered at the incompetence of Long for having recklessly exposed his command, and White, for having created an impossible situation in the first place, but inwardly Buller blamed himself. In despair he sent a cable to White suggesting that if the siege became too testing, he should fire off all his ammunition and surrender to the Boers. Wisely, White ignored him. The first cracks were appearing in the facade of bulldog Buller, and the Home Government decided to send out a senior commander to take direction of the overall strategy out of Buller's hands. They chose Lord Roberts, the leader of the 'Indian Ring', which had long wrangled with the 'Ashanti Ring' of which Buller was a member, and the father of Lieutenant Freddy Roberts, whom Buller had seen struck down at Colenso. Relations between the two were destined to be cool.

For three weeks·both the British and the Boers seemed paralysed by Colenso. Christmas came and went with no change in the strategic situa-

Preparations for the second attempt at relief; Buller's heaviest artillery, the 4.7 in. Naval guns, at Frere camp, December 1899. (SB Bourquin)

Lieutenant General Sir
Charles Warren, commanding
the British 5th Division, was
the senior British commander
in the Spioenkop operations.

tion, but on 6 January 1900 the Boers made a rare attempt to capitalise on their victory and force a way through the defensive perimeter of Ladysmith. Hitherto, most of the fighting around the town had consisted largely of sporadic skirmishes; the Boers shelled the town twice daily, and the British forayed out occasionally to attack their gun emplacements. White's defences were anchored on the southern side on a long, flat-topped, ridge known to the Boers as the Platrand, and to the British as Wagon Hill.

At 0230 on the 6th the Boers mounted an attack on the various British positions on the hill. The fighting was stiff, characterised by close-range fire-fights amongst the boulders, but to the disgust of Botha, who watched but did not command the assault, all but a handful of burghers shied away from fighting hand-to-hand. Reinforcements were rushed out from Ladysmith, and, in the teeth of a sudden summer thunderstorm, three companies of the 1st Devons drove the Boers back at the point of the bayonet, and the attack collapsed.

Clearly the British could not dawdle before the Thukela heights indefinitely. Worried that the Boers were becoming bolder, and that White's resolve might dwindle along with his supplies, Buller decided to have another crack at the Thukela line before Roberts arrived to supersede him. Of course, Buller still faced the same dilemma; where were the Boers vulnerable? Even those critical of his handling of the Colenso battle could come up with no obvious answer.

By the beginning of January, however, Buller had been reinforced by a new Division, the 5th, consisting of two new brigades under the command of Lieutenant-General Sir Charles Warren. He was a Royal Engineer who had enjoyed a colourful career. In 1885 Warren had led an expedition which had seized Bechuanaland from under the nose of the Boers, and he was therefore thought to be sufficiently experienced in southern African affairs to take over from Buller should the latter be killed or wounded.

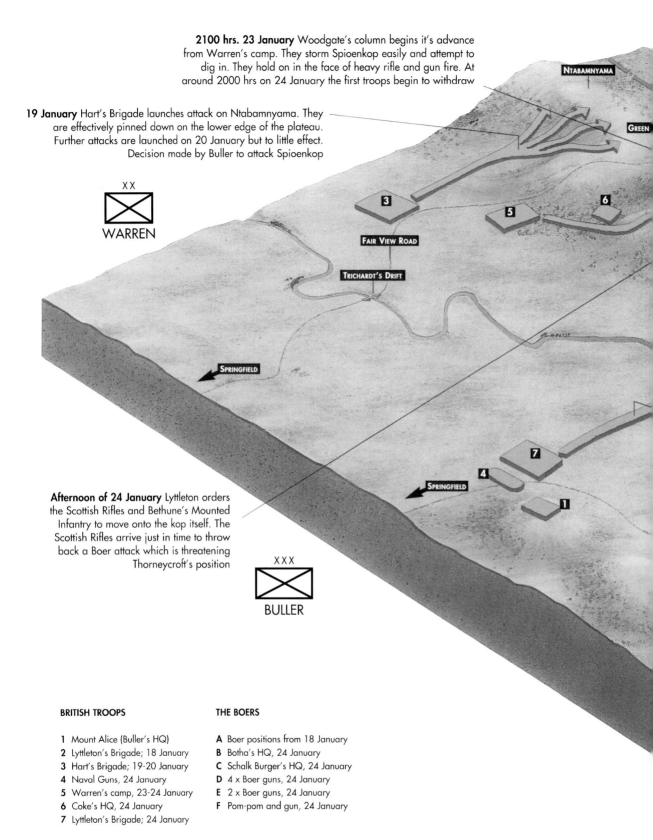

2100 hrs. 23 January Woodgate's column begins it's advance from Warren's camp. They storm Spioenkop easily and attempt to dig in. They hold on in the face of heavy rifle and gun fire. At around 2000 hrs on 24 January the first troops begin to withdraw

19 January Hart's Brigade launches attack on Ntabamnyama. They are effectively pinned down on the lower edge of the plateau. Further attacks are launched on 20 January but to little effect. Decision made by Buller to attack Spioenkop

NTABAMNYAMA

GREEN

X X

WARREN

3

5

6

FAIR VIEW ROAD

TRICHARDT'S DRIFT

SPRINGFIELD

7

4

SPRINGFIELD

1

Afternoon of 24 January Lyttleton orders the Scottish Rifles and Bethune's Mounted Infantry to move onto the kop itself. The Scottish Rifles arrive just in time to throw back a Boer attack which is threatening Thorneycroft's position

X X X

BULLER

BRITISH TROOPS

1 Mount Alice (Buller's HQ)
2 Lyttleton's Brigade; 18 January
3 Hart's Brigade; 19-20 January
4 Naval Guns, 24 January
5 Warren's camp, 23-24 January
6 Coke's HQ, 24 January
7 Lyttleton's Brigade; 24 January

THE BOERS

A Boer positions from 18 January
B Botha's HQ, 24 January
C Schalk Burger's HQ, 24 January
D 4 x Boer guns, 24 January
E 2 x Boer guns, 24 January
F Pom-pom and gun, 24 January

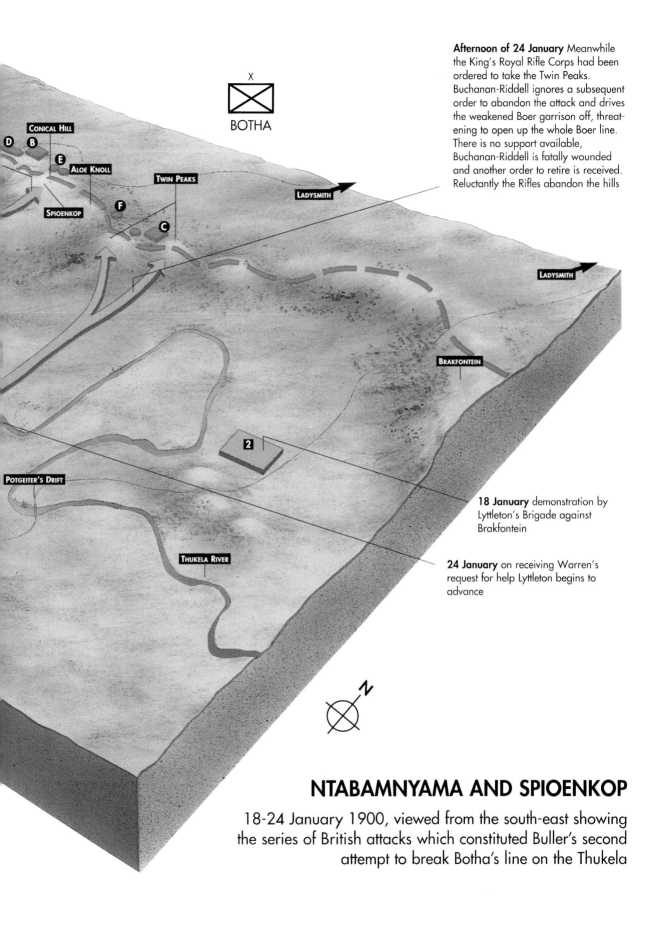

Afternoon of 24 January Meanwhile the King's Royal Rifle Corps had been ordered to take the Twin Peaks. Buchanan-Riddell ignores a subsequent order to abandon the attack and drives the weakened Boer garrison off, threatening to open up the whole Boer line. There is no support available, Buchanan-Riddell is fatally wounded and another order to retire is received. Reluctantly the Rifles abandon the hills

X

BOTHA

CONICAL HILL

D B

E

ALOE KNOLL

TWIN PEAKS

SPIOENKOP

F

C

LADYSMITH

LADYSMITH

BRAKFONTEIN

2

POTGEITER'S DRIFT

18 January demonstration by Lyttleton's Brigade against Brakfontein

24 January on receiving Warren's request for help Lyttleton begins to advance

THUKELA RIVER

N

NTABAMNYAMA AND SPIOENKOP

18-24 January 1900, viewed from the south-east showing the series of British attacks which constituted Buller's second attempt to break Botha's line on the Thukela

Warren had something of an original mind – he was an amateur archaeologist, and he had served a spell as Commissioner for Police in London, during which time he had failed to catch 'Jack The Ripper' – but his temperament varied between the bluff and the acerbic. Buller undoubtedly resented his presence, but with Warren's reinforcements to back him up, Buller felt able to take on Louis Botha once more.

For his second attempt to relieve Ladysmith, Buller reverted to the plan which he had abandoned on the eve of Colenso. Fifteen miles upstream from Colenso, there were two potential crossing points, Potgeiter's Drift and, three miles further west, Trichardt's Drift. Tracks from both wound through the hills on the north bank and thence to Ladysmith, less than 20 miles beyond. Buller hoped that Botha's line would be stretched too thin to cover these heights in depth, whilst a choice of drifts would make it easier for him to cross the river. Had he been able to move swiftly and catch the Boers off-guard, he might have been right, but when he moved out of Frere on 10 January his force of five infantry brigades, a cavalry brigade, eight field batteries, ten naval guns and 650 transport wagons was only too apparent to the Boers on the hills opposite.

Potgeiter's Drift was commanded on the south bank by a hill known as Mount Alice, and Dundonald's cavalry, riding ahead, secured it without opposition. There was an old civilian ferry at the drift itself, and this, too, the British captured. A way across the troublesome Thukela was now at hand, and when he arrived Buller established his headquarters at Mount Alice, and surveyed the hills on the far bank. The same range of rocky ridges extended in an unbroken line from the foothills of the Drakensberg, clearly visible now to the west, all the way to Colenso and beyond.

A track crossing at Potgeiter's ran over a high shoulder directly to Buller's front; this was a hill known as Brakfontein, and the Boers had entrenched it as soon as they had discerned the direction of Buller's advance. A further track – dignified with the name 'Fair View Road' – crossed at Trichardt's Drift upstream and climbed over a plateau known to the Africans as Ntabamnyama. Between Ntabamnyama and Brakfontein lay a series of steep koppies, dominated in the centre by Spioenkop.

Buller's plan was to piece the Boer lines at both points. He ordered Warren to take his division across Trichardt's Drift, whilst he himself would remain at Potgeiter's. Warren was to make a rapid attack on Ntabamnyama, clearing the Fair View Road, then advancing to his right, behind the hills, thereby threatening the Boer positions on Brakfontein. At that point Buller planned to attack in strength across Potgeiter's. Threatened in their flank and rear, Buller hoped that the Boers would not stand before him, and he would be able to relieve Ladysmith by the Potgeiter's road.

In theory, Buller's plan was probably sound enough, but it depended for its success on Warren being able to clear the Boers off Ntabamnyama, and quite why Buller left this important task to his subordinate has never been satisfactorily explained. In the event, the plan misfired because Warren took so long to move his men into position that the Boers had time to reinforce their flimsy breastworks on the Ntabamnyama plateau. Warren believed that the key to success in battle was adequate preparation, but it took him two days to get into position, during which time the Boers heavily reinforced Ntabamnyama. At one point, Dundonald's cavalry brigade, scouting far to the left, easily brushed aside a small party of Boers at a farm called Acton Homes, and Dundonald realised that he had successfully outflanked the Boer line. When he sent a message to Warren urging him to follow up this success, his commander, worried that the cavalry might over-reach themselves, curtly ordered him to withdraw.

Warren finally began his attack on Ntabamnyama on 19 January. It began well enough, the infantry clearing the lower slopes, and advancing steadily towards the crest. When they reached the apparent summit, however, they found that it was merely the bottom edge of a sloping plateau, and that the Boers were secure at the top. To advance further exposed them to a concentrated field of fire, and for the most part they withdrew to the comparative safety of the lower edge. They hung on throughout the night, and renewed the attack in the morning, but without any significant success. Buller, who had watched the attack from Mount Alice with growing frustration, rode over to confer with Warren, but still refused to exert his authority and take over direction of the attack. In a testy conversation Warren grumbled that Ntabamnyama could never be taken unless the British also held Spioenkop, which dominated it on the right, and Buller impatiently agreed. Thus, without any great thought of the consequences, the British resolved to embark on a battle which would prove the most disastrous in the war so far.

THE BATTLE OF SPIOENKOP

From the summit of Spioenkop the views are stunning. The pinnacles and crags of the Drakensberg in the west are tinged with purple in the afternoon light, and to the east Natal is spread out like a rolling green carpet, the sun catching on the tin roofs of Ladysmith less than 20 miles away. It was from this hill that the Boer Voortrekkers first gazed out on what seemed to them a promised land in the 1830s – that's why they called it *Spioenkop* (Look-Out Hill). The hill itself is a whale-backed ridge, running roughly south-west to north-east, and 1470 ft above the river at its highest point. Spurs run out to the north and east, culminating in rocky knolls known as Conical Hill and Aloe Knoll respectively. On the northern side the hill sloped gently down to the plain, but to the south the approaches are steep. Saddles of land connected it to Groenkop (Green Hill), and thence to Ntabamnyama to the north west, and to two jutting hills known as the Twin Peaks to the east. It was quite clearly a dominant position, although neither Warren nor Buller seemed to have any clear idea of what troops might do on the hill when they got there; when asked this

Major General J Talbot-Coke, commander of the 10th Brigade, and nominal commander during the Spioenkop operations.

RIGHT *'Majuba! Majuba!' Thorneycroft's Mounted Infantry take Spioenkop at the point of the bayonet.*

LEFT *The King's Own Royal Lancasters crossing a drift on their way to the front before Spioenkop. (King's Own Royal Lancasters)*

question, Buller merely replied that they would have to 'stay there'. From the beginning the Spioenkop expedition displayed all the lack of purpose which had characterised Majuba 19 years before.

The task of seizing Spioenkop was given to Colonel Coke, of Warren's 10th Brigade, although since Coke was recovering from a broken leg, the actual assault would be led by Major-General E R P Woodgate, another veteran of the Zulu War. Woodgate's column consisted of 1700 men from his own Lancashire Brigade – the 2nd Lancashire Fusiliers, six companies of the 2nd King's Own Royal Lancasters, and two of the South Lancashires. They were supported by 200 men from Thorneycroft's Mounted Infantry, the *uitlander* regiment which had undergone it's baptism of fire at Hlangwane, and half a company of Royal Engineers. A battery of light

TOP *Officers of the Lancashire Fusiliers in January 1900. Note that even by this date most of them are carrying rifles. This battalion suffered heavily at Spioenkop. (SB Bourquin)*

ABOVE *Colonel Alec Thorneycroft (centre) and officers of his Mounted Infantry, photographed before the Spioenkop disaster.*

ABOVE *Spioenkop, photographed shortly after the battle. Aloe Knoll is just visible below the line of the summit, with the spur leading to the Twin Peaks at right foreground and Conical Hill right background. The British held the ground on the left of the picture, the Boers that on the right. (SB Bourquin)*

RIGHT *The summit photographed not long after the war. The main trench on the right of the British line is still clearly visible, looking towards Aloe Knoll (left background) and the Twin Peaks beyond. (Transvaal Archive Depot)*

mountain guns was supposed to accompany the column, but it was still several miles to the rear; sandbags were also prepared, but these were left behind because of their weight. Woodgate expected to be reinforced with artillery and machine-guns once the summit had been secured.

Woodgate's column began its advance from Warren's camp, below Ntabamnyama, at 2100 on the 23rd. Two African guides had been appointed to lead them, but they were lost in the confusion, and the column was led up instead by Colonel Alec Thorneycroft, who had spent the day studying the route through his field glasses – not the last time the British would depend on Thorneycroft's resourcefulness that day. The column toiled up a steep ridge in the inky blackness, halting now and then to check the way, whilst the men remained as silent as possible. As they reached the lip of the summit, Thorneycroft deployed his men into line, and they heard their first challenge from Boer sentries on the top – 'Wie's daar?' – 'Who's there?' Thorneycroft replied with the British password, 'Waterloo', a signal for his men to throw themselves to the ground.

The Boers opened fire with a fusillade of Mauser fire, most of which passed harmlessly overhead, and when they heard the click of fresh clips being loaded, Thorneycroft's men rose up and charged forward shouting 'Majuba! Majuba!' One burgher was caught on the bayonet, and the rest promptly fled. As the rest of Woodgate's column came up, they let out three cheers, the pre-arranged signal to let Warren know the summit was in British hands.

BRITISH

Commander
LIEUTENANT-GENERAL WARREN

Woodgate's (11th) Brigade
2nd Royal Lancaster Regiment
2nd Lancashire Fusiliers
1st South Lancashire Regiment
1st York and Lancaster Regiment

Lyttleton's (4th) Brigade
2nd Scottish Rifles
3rd King's Royal Rifle Corps
1st Durham Light Infantry
1st Rifle Brigade

Coke's (10th) Brigade
2nd Somersetshire Light Infantry
2nd Dorsetshire Regiment
2nd Middlesex Regiment

Mounted Brigade (Dundonald)
1st Royal Dragoons
Mounted Infantry
One Squadron, Natal Police
One Squadron, Natal Carbineers
One Squadron, Imperial Light Infantry
Bethune's Mounted Infantry
Thorneycroft's Mounted Infantry
South African Light Horse.

Notes – Not all of these Brigades were engaged on 24 January 1900 in their entirety (e.g. Dundonald's). Only those Brigades which were involved in the fighting on that day have been listed; Hart's and Hildyard's Brigades remained in position below Ntabamnyama but did not join the attack on Spioenkop. The attack on Spioenkop was supported by the fire of two 4.7 in. and two 12-pdr. Naval guns from Mount Alice. Some British artillery from the Brigades below Ntabamnyama also shelled the western approaches to Spioenkop.

THE BOERS

Commander
COMMANDANT LOUIS BOTHA

The Carolina Commando (Commandant Hendrik Prinsloo) and Pretoria Commando (Commandant Daniel Opperman), bore the brunt of the assault on the kop.
The Krugersdorp, Boksburg, Utrecht and Heidelburg commandos, and German volunteer corps, were in position along the Ntabamnyama and Spioenkop heights; elements of these also joined the attack, as did a number of volunteers from other commandos stationed elsewhere.

2 x 75mm Krupp guns
2 x 75mm Creusot guns
1 x Maxim-Nordenfeldt 'pom-pom pom'.

Twin Peaks Sector
(Commandant Schalk Burger)
Rustenburg Commando, elements of Carolina and Heidelburg Commandos.

1 x Maxim-Nordenfeldt 'pom-pom pom'
1 x 75mm Krupp gun.

The summit of Spioenkop had been held by just 15 men from the Vryheid commando, who had been so caught by surprise that they fled down the northern side of the hill crying out 'Die Engelse is op die kop!' ('The English are up the hill!'). In the first few moments, they spread panic amongst the Boer camps behind the hill.

Woodgate, meanwhile, had placed his men on the summit. Major Massey of the Engineers paced out a line on what appeared to be the crest, though it was still dark, and as dawn broke the summit was obscured by a dense mist. The men then began to dig a trench three or four hundred yards long across the top of Spioenkop, with either end curled back to refuse the flanks. The soil was hard and stony, however, and the men had nothing stronger than their own entrenching tools, and it proved impossible to dig down more than about 18 inches. To compensate, the men piled up boulders in front, but at best the breastwork offered barely adequate

Hand-to-hand combat was rare in the Anglo-Boer War, but the crest-line at Spioenkop was fiercely contested by both sides.

The height of the battle — this sketch gives a vivid impression of the cramped and chaotic conditions among the trenches on the summit, although the officer on the right would not have survived long had he remained in such an exposed position.

protection from rifle fire, and no cover at all from shellfire. Nevertheless, Woodgate had good reason to be pleased with himself, and he sent a signal back to Warren indicating that the hill was firmly in British hands. If Warren had formulated a plan on how best to exploit this advantage, however, he did nothing at this stage to implement it.

The Boers, meanwhile, had pulled themselves together. The news of the British incursion had first reached Commandant Schalk Burger, whose camp lay behind the Twin Peaks. Burger was unnerved by it, and made preparations for retreat, whilst nonetheless ordering Commandant Hendrik Prinsloo of the Carolina Commando to send men onto the hill to investigate the British position. Botha (who had recently established his headquarters behind Green Hill), however, was undaunted, and immediately set out

1300 The Middlesex Regt. under Col. Hill arrive just in time to retake, at bayonet point, a section of the main trench that has just been captured by the Boers. They then deploy to the right of the British Line

The night of 23-24 January, Woodgate's column storm Spioenkop with a bayonet charge. The troops construct a makeshift trench line in the rocky soil

1600 Bethune's Mounted Infantry and the Scottish Rifles reach the summit as Hill's Middlesex men are being driven back. The Rifles rapidly restore the situation

D

SPIC

2

3

4

The heavy fire makes it impossible to hold the crest line and the British are forced to fall back to the main trench (2-5) by 1200

As the mist clears Woodgate pushes forward parties of soldiers to seize the true crest (1) just in time for them to meet the Carolina Commando coming up the hill

6

0830 as mist burns off the British are increasingly exposed to shell fire and flanking fire from Aloe Knoll

X

WOODGATE/THORNYCROFT

THE SUMMIT OF SPIOENKOP

2100 hrs. 23 January-2000 hrs. 24 January, 1900. Viewed from south-east showing the initial British attack and occupation of the summit, and the Boer counterattacks and gunfire

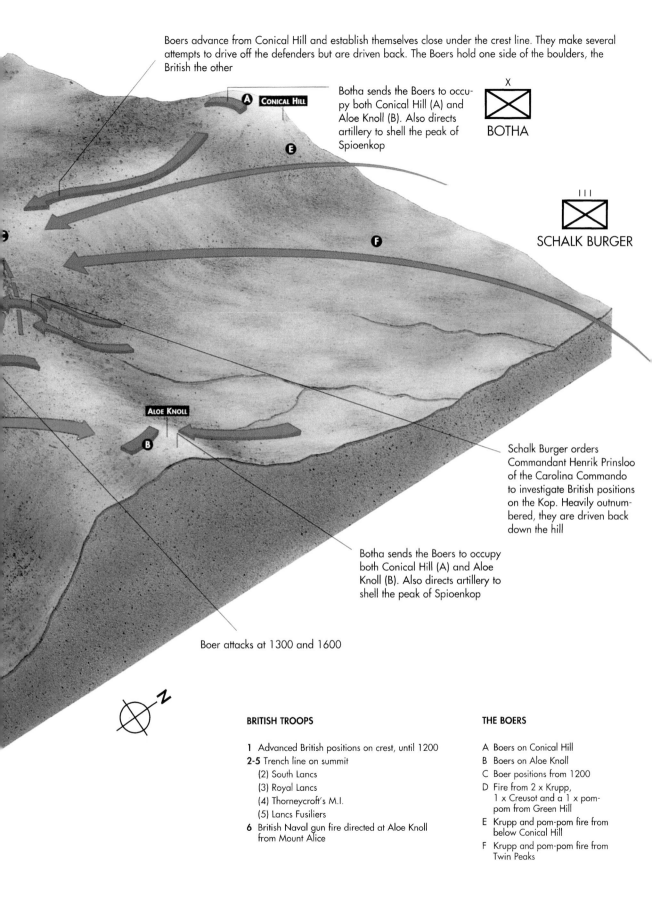

Boers advance from Conical Hill and establish themselves close under the crest line. They make several attempts to drive off the defenders but are driven back. The Boers hold one side of the boulders, the British the other

Botha sends the Boers to occupy both Conical Hill (A) and Aloe Knoll (B). Also directs artillery to shell the peak of Spioenkop

A CONICAL HILL

E

F

X

BOTHA

III

SCHALK BURGER

ALOE KNOLL

B

Schalk Burger orders Commandant Henrik Prinsloo of the Carolina Commando to investigate British positions on the Kop. Heavily outnumbered, they are driven back down the hill

Botha sends the Boers to occupy both Conical Hill (A) and Aloe Knoll (B). Also directs artillery to shell the peak of Spioenkop

Boer attacks at 1300 and 1600

N

BRITISH TROOPS

1 Advanced British positions on crest, until 1200
2-5 Trench line on summit
   (2) South Lancs
   (3) Royal Lancs
   (4) Thorneycroft's M.I.
   (5) Lancs Fusiliers
6 British Naval gun fire directed at Aloe Knoll from Mount Alice

THE BOERS

A Boers on Conical Hill
B Boers on Aloe Knoll
C Boer positions from 1200
D Fire from 2 x Krupp, 1 x Creusot and a 1 x pom-pom from Green Hill
E Krupp and pom-pom fire from below Conical Hill
F Krupp and pom-pom fire from Twin Peaks

along the Boer line, urging his men to screw up their courage and make a counter attack. Prinsloo had sent just 25 men forward to try to scale the summit, and they clambered up the north-eastern slopes, following the line of a gully that scoured the nek between Spioenkop and Aloe Knoll. They were just below the summit when the mist lifted, and the curtain rose on the great drama of the battle of Spioenkop.

As soon as visibility cleared, Woodgate realised that he had miscalculated dreadfully; although the ground sloped away in front of his trench, he did not in fact command the crest, since the hill shelved steeply a mere hundred yards in front of him, and dropped into dead ground. This was all his position commanded; beyond that the Boers could scramble up the slope out of reach of his fire. He immediately pushed out parties to seize the line of boulders which marked the rim of the true crest, but these men were scarcely in position when they encountered the Carolina men coming in the opposite direction, and the first-fire fights of the day broke out. The Carolina men, badly outnumbered, fell back down the hill, but met the rest of their commando coming up. Prinsloo rallied them with the stern injunction 'Burgers, we are going to confront the enemy and will not all return. Do your duty and have faith in the Lord'.

A poignant pair of photographs – the top shot shows two sergeants of the King's Own Lancasters before Spioenkop, whilst the one below shows one of them – the man on the right – lying dead on the summit of Spioenkop. The original caption to this picture reads simply, 'The last of my poor chum'. (King's Own Museum, Lancaster)

Botha, meanwhile, had galvanised the Boers. Having no knowledge of the true lie of the land, Woodgate had made no attempt to occupy either the Conical Hill or Aloe Knoll, and Botha sent the Boers scampering up the slopes to seize them before the British realised their mistake. The loss of Aloe Knoll was particularly serious to the British, since it was almost on a level with Woodgate's line on the right of the crest, and offered the chance for enfilading fire. Worse, Botha moved his artillery and directed it to fire on the summit. Two 75mm Creusots, a Krupp and a pom-pom on the northern slopes of Ntabamnyama, behind Green Hill, altered their position to fire at Spioenkop, whilst a Krupp gun and pom-pom opened up from below Conical Hill. To the east, another Krupp was dragged into position below the western Twin Peak, whilst a pom-pom was placed on the saddle below Aloe Knoll. By the time the mist had burnt off completely, at about 0830,

British dead tossed haphazardly by a direct hit from a
Boer shell on Spioenkop. The
inadequacy of the trench as
protection could scarcely be
better demonstrated. The
view is along the right of the
line, with Aloe Knoll and
Twin Peaks in the back-
ground. (Transvaal Archives
Depot)

Woodgate found his position exposed to a deadly semi-circle of fire.

Nevertheless, the British remained confident throughout the early morning. Boers making their way up the northern slopes crouched close under the crest line, and tried several times to dislodge the defenders there, only to be driven back with bayonet or clubbed rifle. Soon the British held one side of the boulders and the Boers the other, and any man rising to fire risked being shot at close range. The main trench remained secure, however, despite being increasingly exposed to shell-fire, against which there was no protection. A Boer signaller, Louis Bothma, climbed most of the way up the slope and directed the fire from just below the summit, ensuring a remarkable degree of accuracy. At the height of the battle Boer shells were exploding on the summit at the rate of seven a minute, often just yards ahead of the Boer positions, and this punishing rate was main-tained throughout much of the day.

Woodgate himself was an early casualty of this fire. Colonel Blomfield of the Lancashire Fusiliers drew his attention to Boers coming up the slope, and Woodgate had just raised his head to look when he was struck by a shrapnel ball above the right eye. He was taken down the hill on a stretch-er, and lingered in agony for several weeks before he died. Blomfield him-self was wounded shortly after, and there then began a grim farce over the question of who should command on Spioenkop. The most senior officers on the hill were Colonel Crofton of the Royal Lancasters and Colonel Thorneycroft; as a regular, Crofton naturally assumed command.

When news reached Warren that Woodgate was injured, he sent a mes-sage ordering the brigade commander, Coke, to the summit to take com-mand in person. It was a long climb up, however, and Coke was overtak-en by events. Heliograph messages from the summit were clearly visible to Buller on Mount Alice, however. Indeed, Buller could see them better than Warren, below Ntabamnyama, and he signalled to Warren suggesting that Thorneycroft – 'a good fighting officer' – be placed in command. Warren agreed, and sent a messenger to inform Thorneycroft, but without inform-ing Coke, who was still on his way up to the summit.

On top of Spioenkop, meanwhile, the situation had deteriorated. The day was growing hotter by the hour, and the British troops were begin-

Arguably the most famous – and one of the most moving – photographs of the Anglo-Boer War; British dead collected together for burial in one of the trenches on Spioenkop, two days after the battle. (SB Bourquin)

ning to suffer for lack of water. Boer shellfire played along the main trench, killing, maiming and mutilating, and tossing bodies in amongst the living. No attempt had been made by Warren to exploit whatever advantage had been gained by seizing the hill. The British might have been able to hold their own against the Boer riflemen, but they had no reply to the incessant shell-fire. Warren's artillery, below Ntabamnyama, shelled the area around Conical Hill, hoping to strike at any Boer reinforcements, but for the most part the Boers simply rode around the target area. At one point the naval guns on Mount Alice, spotting an opportunity, opened fire on Aloe Knoll, but Warren, who assumed the whole summit was in British hands, sent an urgent message ordering them to stop, believing they were shelling their own men. By the middle of the morning, Thorneycroft signalled that he was in need of reinforcements.

The tone of Thorneycroft's message took Warren by surprise, and he ordered the Middlesex Regiment and Imperial Light Infantry up from the reserve. He also sent a message to Lyttleton, near Mount Alice, asking him to support the attack. The reinforcements had a grim climb up the shoulder, past lines of wounded and exhausted men being carried down, but they reached the summit just in time to avert a major British crisis.

By late morning, the British had abandoned most of the crest. The flanking fire from Aloe Knoll had made it almost impossible to hold the right of the line, and the men fell back to the main trench. This enabled the Boers to creep further forward, and by about 1300 the Lancashire Fusiliers were suffering severely. Someone raised a white flag, and, after a moment of confusion, a number of Fusiliers ran forward with their hands

up. Thorneycroft, who had been with his own men in the centre, rushed down to intercept them, bellowing at an astonished Boer commandant 'I'm the commandant here; take your men back to Hell sir! I allow no surrenders!' Thorneycroft rallied the Fusiliers around him, but some (over 100 according to Boer sources) nonetheless ran forward to join the Boers, and he was obliged to retire to a rocky outcrop behind the trench. Several Boers slipped into the trench, and part of the main British line was now in enemy hands. At this point, however, Thorneycroft saw the Middlesex Regiment coming up the slope, and he urged them forward, recapturing the trench at the point of the bayonet. The Middlesex, under their commander, Colonel Hill, deployed to the right of the British line, almost as far as the steep drop on the edge of the kop itself.

It seems to have occurred to neither Buller nor Warren that the best way to ease the position on Spioenkop, and perhaps to break through the Boer lines altogether, was to launch an attack elsewhere along the front. Indeed, Botha had stripped both Ntabamnyama and the Twin Peaks of most of their garrisons, and was dangerously vulnerable to any additional attack elsewhere. Only Neville Lyttleton was prepared to risk it; when he received Warren's request for help, he despatched the Scottish Rifles and Bethune's Mounted Infantry to the kop itself, but ordered the King's Royal Rifle Corps (KRRC) – the old 3/60th Rifles, who had suffered at Boer hands in 1881 – to cross at Potgeiter's, and take the Twin Peaks. No sooner had the 60th begun their advance, however, than Lyttleton received a message from Spioenkop suggesting that the Twin Peaks were more strongly held than he thought. He sent a message after the Rifles, ordering them to call off the attack.

However, with old scores to settle, the Colonel of the KRRC, Buchanan-Riddell, discretely ignored Lyttleton's message. They marched across the flats, deployed in line, and scrambled up the boulder-strew slopes of the

The defenders of Spioenkop – a Boer commando on one of the Twin Peaks, January 1900.

Officers of the King's Royal Rifle Corps – the old 3/60th – near Mount Alice. The KRRC captured Twin Peaks, offering the British a rare, and ultimately wasted, chance of victory during the Spioenkop operations. (SB Bourquin)

Twin Peaks. A further order was sent, instructing them to desist, but this too was ignored, and the Rifles drove the weakened Boer garrison off the Twin Peaks. It was too much for Schalk Burger, behind the hills, who ordered the threatened Krupp and pom-pom to withdraw. This brilliant stroke was therefore poised to open up the whole Boer line, but it could not be exploited without support, and Lyttleton sent yet another message ordering the 60th to withdraw. It arrived shortly after Buchanan-Riddell was fatally wounded, and his officers felt it was impossible to ignore orders any longer. Reluctantly they abandoned the hills, retiring back the way they had come. It was dark by the time they reached the drift, and the troops there lit a bonfire to guide them back.

The attack on the Twin Peaks was perhaps the last chance the British had to win the day. On the summit, the Boers had renewed their attack on the British right. Creeping along the steep southern slopes from Aloe Knoll, under cover of the boulders on the crest, a handful of Boers had almost succeeded in outflanking the Middlesex men. Under a heavy fire Hill was forced to abandon his HQ and fall back, and for a moment it looked as if the Boers would be in a position to fire on the rear of Thorneycroft's position in the middle of the line. At the crucial moment, however, reinforcements again saved the day, and the Scottish Rifles, reaching the summit, drove the Boers back.

It was by now late afternoon, and the complicated command question was given a further twist. A fresh Colonel – Cooke, of the Scottish Rifles – was now on Spioenkop, with some claim to seniority. Then Coke arrived briefly on the summit, and, unaware that Warren had appointed Thorneycroft to command there, ordered Colonel Hill of the Middlesex to take command. Coke himself had then retired part of the way down the hill. By now the summit was swept by shell-fire, the units were mixed up, many of the officers were dead and wounded, and the men were suffering from the heat and exhaustion. In these chaotic conditions the command structure was in danger of breaking down completely.

Thorneycroft was feeling increasingly abandoned by his senior officers; his men had hung on with extraordinary courage, but neither Warren nor Buller had supported him. It was no longer clear to him what he could achieve; the arrival of reinforcements had merely exposed more men to the deadly fire-storm, and he feared that a renewal of fighting in the morning would only destroy his command completely. At dusk Thorneycroft consulted his officers, and resolved to abandon Spioenkop. One or two opposed the suggestion, and several others could not be found in the confusion, but most agreed. At about 2000 (after dark) the first troops begun reluctantly to withdraw from the trench and down the hill. On the way they passed Engineers coming up, who had been ordered, at last, to make good the defences. Various individuals, among them Winston Churchill, who had escaped from the Boers after the armoured train fiasco and made his way back to the front, tried to persuade Thorneycroft to stay, but his mind was made up. When Coke, on the lower slopes, heard of the retreat, he tried to signal to Warren for advice, but his signallers found they had no oil in their lamps. By midnight the only British troops left on Spioenkop were the dead and dying.

Ironically, the Boers, too, contemplated giving up the fight that night. They had also suffered terrible casualties, and the shallow breastworks were enough to mask the true extent of the British suffering, thus leaving the Boers with the impression that they had had the worst of the fight. With the onset of darkness, many burghers began to slip away. It wasn't until the early hours that a few brave souls, creeping out to look for injured comrades, realised that the British were no longer in their trenches, and carried the astonishing news to Botha. It was not an opportunity for a man like Botha to miss; by dawn on the 25th the Boers had reoccupied the entire summit.

In the cold grey first light of 25 January, Spioenkop was a terrible sight. The trenches were piled with British dead, many of them horrifically mutilated by shell-fire. Here and there a Boer lay among them, whilst many badly wounded men were scarcely distinguishable from the dead. Helmets, spent cartridge cases and pieces of equipment were strewn everywhere. Botha and Buller agreed a truce, and Boers and British medical personnel alike picked across the battlefield in shocked silence. When the final toll was reckoned, it was found that the British had lost 350 dead, 1000 wounded, and 200 captured. The Boers had lost 75 dead and 150 wounded, a remarkably high casualty rate given their preferred style of warfare, which reflected the desperate nature of the fighting.

AFTER SPIOENKOP

The grim spectacle of long lines of stretcher bearers winding down the track from the summit had a sobering effect on Buller's army. Yet the Spioenkop plan was perhaps not as flawed as later critics suggested; it failed largely through the inability of the British to exploit their advantage quickly enough. For this Warren and Buller must take much of the blame, yet a portion of it was due, too, to the problems posed by a new style of warfare. Because of the communication problems, it was almost impossible for the Generals behind the lines to control the battle once it had begun; another situation which was to become all too familiar in World War 1. This, coupled with the use of smokeless powder, had made it difficult to identify the positions of the Boer artillery, and effectively neutralised the British artillery. Behind the legend of Buller's blundering there lay a painful truth – an army which had learned its craft in the 19th century was having to test it in the fiery crucible of the 20th. It was proving a costly lesson to learn.

Buller reacted gloomily to news of the disaster, for which he held Warren largely responsible. Lord Roberts, Buller's replacement, was now established in Cape Town, and was massing troops to mount a major strike along the railway line towards Kimberley, and then into the Boer heartlands. Roberts cabled Buller ordering him to take no more offensive action, but Buller, worried that the Boers might now be bold enough to mount a further attack on Ladysmith, was determined to break through the Thukela line. On 5 February he shifted the focus of his attack a few miles to the east, to try to force the Brakfontein road by clearing the Vaalkranz ridge to its right. Once more troops were marched across the Thukela, and Lyttleton's Brigade launched a spirited attack on the Boer positions. Although the British gained some ground, the terrain was too broken for them to bring up artillery support, and after hanging on for two days amongst the boulders, Buller reluctantly ordered retreat. He held a council of war amongst his officers, and the decision was taken to call off the attack. It had cost a further 300 casualties.

BREAKTHROUGH

With the failure at Vaalkranz, Buller marched his army once more back to Frere. By now morale amongst his troops was faltering – there were those who spoke of Buller as 'Sir Reverse' and 'The Ferryman of the Thukela' – but even his critics could see no solution to their problems. Trenches, smokeless powder, the storm of fire; all would have to be faced wherever an attack was mounted, and Botha held all the best ground. Except, perhaps, at Colenso. Buller's initial thrust had failed there, but that northward curve of the river, which isolated Hlangwane on the 'British' bank, might yet afford an opportunity. In the two months since the battle of 15 December, Botha had extended his lines considerably to the east of his original position at Colenso village, and the British movements still remained so obvious that he could hardly fail to see where Buller was massing. Yet if the British could get a toe-hold amongst the hills on the southern bank, they might yet be able to force the Boers out of their positions. Spioenkop and Vaalkranz had taught hard lessons, but new tactics were emerging, and they might yet prove effective against Hlangwane. If Buller could seize the hills on the south bank, he could use the Thukela valley, and the gorge through which it flows north of Colenso, to mask a crossing from Botha, and to mass for an attack on a range of ridges beyond.

And that is what he did. On 18 February Lyttleton's Brigade struck out at Cingolo, a ridge to the east of Hlangwane. In an almost text-book attack, the British artillery concentrated its fire on Boer trenches which had been carefully identified beforehand, and the infantry rushed forward, in open order, making good use of cover, and supported by heavy Maxim fire. The Boers, whose resolve was already fragile because the Thukela was in their rear and cut their line of retreat, abandoned the position and fell back. With its flank turned, Hlangwane was easy prey when Buller followed through the next day. By 20 February, the British held the south bank of the river along the stretch north of Colenso.

The next stage was not so easy. Across the river the Boers held a series of ridges which dominated the valley; these the British later christened Wynne's Hill, Hart's Hill, Railway Hill, and, a final bastion, Pieter's Hill. Buller had been worried about these heights back in December, and he could expect them to be doubly dangerous now, but beyond them lay the plain, and the way through to Ladysmith. Over the next two days Buller

Some of the men of the Lancashire Fusiliers who were captured at Spioenkop, under guard en route to Pretoria. (SB Bourquin)

RIGHT *'The Long Ladder of Pain'; bringing British wounded down from the summit of Spioenkop.*

THE BREAKTHROUGH

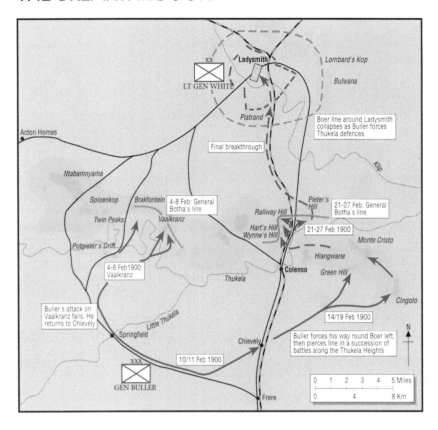

pushed his men across the river by pontoon bridge, and he began his attack on the 22nd. He planned to attack each Boer position in turn, but the attack was not, at first, as concentrated or co-ordinated as he had hoped; the 11th Brigade broached the crest of Wynne's Hill to find, as expected, the Boer positions lying at the top of a gentle scarp above them. In trying to force a way across the open ground they were exposed to the full weight of the Boer fire. They clung on desperately throughout the night, and the next day Hart led the Irish Brigade against Hart's Hill. They had no more luck; Hart himself still rode about recklessly, urging his men into the open and insisting they close up their formations.

The fighting along Wynne's Hill and Hart's Hill lasted for three days, and at the end Buller and Botha agreed a truce to carry off the wounded. If Botha hoped that Buller would abandon the plan, however, he was mistaken, for both Buller and his army were now learning from their mistakes. On 27 February – the anniversary of Majuba – the fighting continued. Buller sent Barton's Brigade into the Thukela valley, where they crossed in dead ground below Pieter's Hill, which commanded the flank of Wynne's and Hart's Hills. Barton's men struggled up the boulder-strewn slope, picking their way through aloes and thorn bush to launch their attack. Buller's guns laid down a creeping barrage – a very innovative tactic – just in front

Men of No 4 Bearer Company photographed during the Spioenkop campaign; to the soldiers these men were known ironically as 'body-snatchers'. (SB Bourquin)

of the advancing infantry, and the Brigade reached the summit of Pieter's plateau. There was a nasty moment when they passed beyond the range of their artillery support, and their initial assaults faltered before the storm of Mauser fire. When, however, another Brigade assault won ground on Railway Hill to the left, the Boer line cracked. Hundreds of burghers began to stream to the rear, and a fierce charge by the 2nd Royal Irish and Dublin Fusiliers cleared the summit of Pieter's. The whole British line advanced, and the Boers collapsed. After eight days of pressure, the Thukela Heights were at last in Buller's hands – the door to Ladysmith lay open.

THE RELIEF OF LADYSMITH

The Boer retreat after Pieter's Hill verged on a rout. The men fleeing the Thukela line spread the news amongst the laagers around Ladysmith, and the entire Boer force began to stream back the way it had come. They made no stand on the outskirts of the town; indeed, there was not time, even, to rescue the stores they had accumulated by rail at Elandslaagte, and these they simply set alight. Buller, to the eternal regret of his cavalry, refused the opportunity to pursue them. Instead, he concentrated on making a formal entry into Ladysmith.

Some of Buller's cavalry eagerly pushed forward into the town on the evening of the 28th, but the grand march-past and formal entry did not take place until 3 March. White and Buller shook hands in front of the

Town Hall whilst soldiers and civilians alike, besieged and relievers, cheered and tossed their hats in the air. The siege had lasted 118 days, and in the last month the strain and lack of food and medical supplies had begun to tell on the defenders. White had lost 18 Officers and 193 men killed in action, and 600 soldiers and civilians through disease; it had cost Buller nearly twice as many men to dig him out. The Boer losses for the whole campaign probably amounted to about 400 or 500 men.

The relief of Ladysmith represented a general and dramatic improvement in the British fortunes. Only a few days before, Roberts had won a spectacular victory at Paadeberg on the western front; across the country the Boers seemed to be in retreat, and the British colonies were free again. Once the jubilation was over, Buller concentrated in clearing the rest of Natal, and over the next few months he drove the Boers back to the Drakensberg in a series of successful actions. Old 'Sir Reverse' had learned his lesson, and nothing could stand before him.

Yet it was on the western front where the Anglo-Boer War was really won, as the British had always known it would be. Roberts gradually, sometimes no more imaginatively than Buller, drove the Boers back before

British troops crossing the Thukela by pontoon bridge during the attacks along the Thukela Heights in February 1900.

A Naval 12-pdr in action at Vaalkranz; the shell can be seen exploding on the skyline in the distance.

his steamroller advance, and on 13 March he entered the Free State Capital Bloemfontein. Three months later Pretoria fell, and Kruger fled to Holland, where he died in exile.

The capture of Pretoria marked the end of the formal phase of the fighting, but the war itself had almost two years to run. Many Boers took to the mountains and the bush in small bands, and waged a protracted and increasingly bitter guerrilla campaign. Roberts responded by forcibly removing Boer civilians from the countryside in an attempt to cut the support out from under these 'bitter-enders', but the inefficiency with which they were cared for in concentration camps led to a dreadful death toll through disease and malnutrition. It was not until 31 May 1902 that the last of the Boer guerrillas were battered and starved into submission, leaving a legacy of ill-feeling which cast a shadow long into the 20th century.

THE BATTLEFIELDS TODAY

The modern town of Ladysmith is an obvious place for anyone interested in the Natal campaign to start a visit to the battlefields. Now a quiet town largely catering for the local agricultural community, Ladysmith still wears an air of its Imperial past, and relics of the Siege abound. The town hall, damaged by Boer shell-fire, still stands in the high street, though the damage was repaired in 1923; two 6.3 in. howitzers, used by the garrison, now stand outside. Nearby, the excellent Siege Museum contains exhibits, artefacts, displays and dioramas relating not only to the fighting, but to the civilian experience during the siege. It is also an excellent source of guide-books and pamphlets to the battlefields nearby. The hills surrounding the town are still capped with obelisks commemorating the fighting, and on the largest of them, the Platrand, there is a neat British graveyard, and a more modern expressive burgher monument, the concrete

A modern photograph of the Colenso battlefield, taken from below the heights, looking towards the British position; the loop in the Thukela where Hart's Brigade was trapped is marked by bush in the middle-distance.

The summit of Spioenkop, showing the precipitous southern slopes, and the boulders which run around the crest line.

'Hands of Grief', where the remains of nearly 400 Boers who died fighting in Natal were later collected together and interred. The main road to the south still crosses the Thukela at Colenso, though the modern road runs to the west of the old track, and cuts through the heights on the north bank below Grobelaars' Kop. Some of Botha's stone emplacements are still visible from the road – the most obvious ones are probably dummies, constructed to draw British fire – whilst the loop where Hart's Brigade came to grief can be traced by a curve of dark undergrowth on the flats below. The spot where Long's guns came to grief is rather disappointing, however, as it now lies on the outskirts of Colenso town, and the view towards Fort Wylie and the Boer positions is obscured by the chimneys of a power-station. Nevertheless, the site of the individual guns has been marked out with concrete blocks. Indeed, the gradual expansion of Colenso itself seemed to be threatening the position of some of the British war-graves, and in the 1960s the dead were exhumed, and reintered south of the town in the Clouston Field of Rememberence. Although this move has proved a controversial one, the Clouston site is not inappropriate, being the spot from which Buller watched the fight. From here one can obtain a good view of the battlefield as it appeared to the British; a low-lying plain, broken by the obscure course of the river, and bordered by the far line of hills held by the Boers.

Spioenkop is arguably the best preserved and best presented battlefield in Natal. Today the Thukela has been dammed below Trichardt's Drift, and the resultant lake has swallowed up the site of Warren's crossing. The area around the lake is owned by the Natal Parks Board, and is a wildlife-sanctuary; it is well-sign-posted and offers the visitor to the area cheap log-cabin accommodation. A small museum commemorating the battle can be found in the Parks Board offices. It is difficult, however, to ascend Spioenkop from the British side, and the modern approach is now on the Boer side, where an unobtrusive road has been built right up to the top. A walking trail has been well-marked around the summit, and a useful guide-book identifies the features.

The trail begins at a point over-looking the ridge by which Woodgate's men ascended, follows the trenchline across to the crest, and then round towards the Boer positions on the northern slopes. For much of its length the trench-line is clearly visible, a shallow scraping and low line of boulders in the scrubby grass. The summit is littered with monuments to both sides; most poignant of all are the British mass-graves, instantly recognisable from the photographs of the time; they are filled in now and marked by walls of white-washed stones. It's a short walk out to Aloe Knoll, overlooked by the thrusting bulk of the Twin Peaks beyond; to reach the Peaks themselves, however, requires quite a hike across country.

The battlefields of the Thukela Heights, where Buller finally forced his way through to Ladysmith, are less often visited, and best approached with the services of a local guide (the Siege Museum will be happy to offer advice). In the tangled web of ridges and narrow valleys, it is all too easy to lose a sense of direction, and to see why this topography, dominated by an intelligent enemy, so often frustrated British attempts to master it. Off the beaten track, Wynne's Hill, Hart's Hill, Railway Hill and Pieter's Hill seem to have changed little since the fighting of almost a century ago; they too are dotted with graves, monuments, and long abandoned trenches, which are still kept in good repair. On these rocky hill-sides, the ghosts of British soldiers and Boer farmers still seem to linger in the quiet shadows, hidden away from the harsh searching glare of the African sunlight and modernity.

CHRONOLOGY THE LADYSMITH CAMPAIGN

11 October 1899 – Transvaal ultimatum expires, Anglo-Boer War begins. Boer forces invade British colonies in South Africa.

14 October – General Buller departs the UK with advanced guard of Army Corps.

20 October – Boers surround Dundee in northern Natal – BATTLE OF TALANA. Boers defeated, but British commander, General Penn-Symons, mortally wounded.

21 October – Lt.Gen. White's troops sally out from Ladysmith to clear Boers threatening line of communication to Dundee; BATTLE OF ELANDSLAAGTE.

22 October – British troops begin retreat from Dundee.

24 October – White again attempts to clear line to Dundee; BATTLE OF RIETFONTEIN.

26 October – Yule's troops from Dundee reach Ladysmith.

30 October – 'Mournful Monday' – White's unsuccessful attempt to clear Boers from around Ladysmith – BATTLES OF NICHOLSON'S NEK AND PEPWORTH HILL.

31 October – Buller arrives in Cape Town, followed over the next week by the Army Corps.

15 November – Botha destroys armoured train near Chieveley. Leading elements of Army Corps (Barton's and Hildyard's Brigades) arrive in Natal.

22 November – Barton and Hildyard check Boer advance in inconclusive BATTLE OF WILLOW GRANGE.

6 December – Buller arrives at Frere.

10 December – British troops in Cape Colony defeated at BATTLE OF STORMBERG.

11 December – British troops on western front defeated at BATTLE OF MAGERSFONTEIN.

15 December – Buller's first attempt to breach Thukela line; BATTLE OF COLENSO.

6 January 1900 – Boer attacks on British positions around Ladysmith; BATTLES OF WAGON HILL AND CAESAR'S CAMP (PLATRAND).

10 January – Arrival at Frere of Lt.Gen. Warren's 5th Division.

11 January – advance towards Potgeiter's Drift.

19/20 January – Warren's attack on Ntabamnyama.

24 January – BATTLE OF SPIOENKOP.

5/7 February – Buller attempts to force Brakfontein ridge; BATTLE OF VAALKRANZ.

British artillery on Mount Alice – 12-pdr Naval guns – support the Ntabamnyama and Spioenkop operations. Ntabamnyama is on the left, whilst Spioenkop is centre right, with one of the Twin Peaks on the skyline beyond.

12 February – Buller's army returns to Frere.

14 February – start of action against Thukela Heights.

18 February – British secure south bank of Thukela after capture of Cingolo, Monte Cristo and Hlangwane heights.

22 February – first attack across Thukela, BATTLE OF WYNNE'S HILL.

23/24 February – attack on Hart's Hill.

25 February – Buller and Botha agree armistice to tend wounded.

27 February – BATTLE OF PIETER'S HILL AND RAILWAY HILL; British break through Boer lines on Thukela.

28 February – First troops from Buller's army enter Ladysmith.

1 March – Buller himself enters Ladysmith for the first time.

3 March 1900 – Buller's formal entry and march-past into Ladysmith – the end of the siege.

A GUIDE TO
FURTHER READING

As the largest of the 19th century British Colonial campaigns, the Anglo-Boer War has produced an extensive body of literature. The very scale of the war, however, sometimes undermines the value of much of this work; some of the volumes of personal memoirs, particularly those produced 20 or 30 years after the event, are so general as to hold appeal to only the most dedicated scholar, whilst many of the more recent histories lack thorough tactical analysis. Undoubtedly the most comprehensive contemporary history is Leo Amery's seven-volume *Times History Of The War In South Africa* (1900-1909), which includes a detailed description of every battle of the war, most of them illustrated with excellent maps. Amery had covered part of the war as a journalist, and his history is based on a rich variety of official and unofficial sources; it is, however, fiercely partisan, since the author was deeply committed to the cause of Army reform. Amery castigates Buller, rather unfairly, as the epitome of all that was worst in the British Army of the 1890s — conservative, hierarchical, beaurocratic and unimaginative. This bias must be born in mind, particularly with regard to the Natal campaign. Other contemporary histories, such as Conan Doyle's *The Great Boer War* (1900-1902) are best read for the flavour and feelings of the times. British magazines which covered the war, such as *With The Flag To Pretoria*, and its sequel, *After Pretoria — The Guerrilla War*, and *Black And White Budget*, can often be found in bound volumes, and, whilst they lack perspective and contain occasional errors of reporting, they do include an extraordinary wealth of illustrative material.

For a modern one-volume history, Thomas Pakenham's *The Boer War* (1979) is justly acclaimed for its extraordinary breadth of scholarship and fair-mindedness. Pakenham attempts to justify Buller's actions in the Thukela campaign, and is therefore an essential corrective to Amery. W. Baring Pemberton's *Battles Of The Boer War* (1964) provides a crisp analysis of the major battles. Kenneth Griffith's *Thank God We Kept The Flag Flying* (1974) is a highly personal view of the siege of Ladysmith, rich in the spirit of the times.

Boer accounts of the war written or translated into English are still rather thin on the ground, but the classic of them all is undoubtedly Denys Reitz's *Commando; A Boer Journal of the Boer War* (1929). Reitz was 17 when he joined the Pretoria commando, and he served throughout the Natal campaign, including Spioenkop, where he was amongst those who struggled to win the crest-line. He remained in the field throughout the war, and his reminiscences have a freshness and poignancy equalled by few others on either side. Winston Churchill's accounts of his adventures can be found in *London To Ladysmith Via Pretoria* (1900) and *My Early Life* (1943).

A resume of British army uniform and equipment of the period can be found in Michael Barthorp's Osprey Men-at-Arms title, *British Army On Campaign 1816-1902 (4); 1882-1902*. Similar treatment of the Boer forces is in Ian Knight's MAA *Queen Victoria's Enemies (1); Southern Africa*. Two very useful articles on the Boer forces, written by Erwin Schmidl and illustrated by Peter Dennis, appeared in issues 23 and 26 of *Military Illustrated* magazine.

WARGAMING COLENSO AND SPIOENKOP

To date, the Anglo-Boer War has not achieved the popularity among wargamers that other British colonial campaigns, notably the Zulu and Sudan Wars, have enjoyed. This is a shame, since the period offers an intriguing mixture of the 19th century 'small war' and so-called 'modern' warfare, and the period is well represented by a number of excellent 15mm and 25mm figure ranges.

With all wargaming scenarios based on historical events, a successful re-enactment depends on careful pre-game planning. Anyone seeking to recreate the conditions of the battle of Colenso must not only duplicate the essentials of the terrain – an open board with a winding river at one end, and beyond it hills – but also something of the British confusion. The game should be ideally played by a number of British players, representing the various Brigade commanders. Their objectives should be set by an umpire, and these objectives might contain a certain element of deliberate confusion. Players might be told to advance towards or secure various objectives, but not have those objectives clearly identified.

A player representing Hart, for example, might be told to advance towards a given point on the river, only to be told on reaching it that the drift he seeks lies elsewhere. Colonel Long might be ordered to take up a position at a certain distance from the nearest Boer positions, but left to his own judgement to decide where those positions are. To replicate the concealed nature of the Boer positions, these should be marked on a map by the umpire, but not revealed to the British players until they have been convincingly sought out by artillery-fire, or are threatened by the close proximity of advancing infantry.

Since the vast majority of British soldiers who fought at Colenso never saw a Boer throughout the entire engagement, it should be perfectly possible for the umpire to control Boer fire without placing a figure on the board during the game! Ideally, the British players should be left groping for an objective, and under fire from an enemy they cannot locate; the true test of their generalship will be whether they nonetheless manage to force a way across the river and secure a toe-hold If so, it might reasonably be held that the Boers have lost their objective.

Spioenkop is a rather more difficult battle to represent, since its particular character owes a good deal to both the broader tactics employed, and to the individual close-quarter struggles on the kop itself. For a conventional wargame, the terrain should ideally stretch from Ntabamnyama on one side to the Twin Peaks on the other. The game should perhaps begin with the British entrenched on the summit of Spioenkop, and the Boers scattered in pockets along the remaining hills and at the foot of the kop. To duplicate the confusion of the early-morning mist, the Boer player should be allowed a number of free moves, to concentrate his forces and begin the attack on the kop. For the Boer player, therefore, the objective should be to drive the British off the hill; for the British player it should simply be to hang on.

To represent the unco-ordinated interference from the senior British commanders, the British player might be reinforced at random, and sudden bursts of off-table artillery-fire be directed at arbitrarily chosen sectors of the table, which may or may not contain Boer figures. At the discretion of the umpire, further British troops may be introduced onto the table without warning, to attack one of the other terrain features – the Twin Peaks or Ntabamnyama. To add extra spice to this attack, each move should be accompanied by a throw of the dice. When a predetermined number is rolled, the attack should be called off, and the figures marched back to their base-line. Will this attack, like Lyttleton's, seize an important objective only to abandon it at the crucial moment? Will it, indeed, be called off before it has begun – or will it be successful, and force the Boer player to divert some of his attention from Spioenkop, thereby opening the way for a British victory?

An alternative way to represent the battle might be to use a small table area to represent the summit of Spioenkop itself. Using a set of 'large skirmish' rules and an individual figure approach, the British should be deployed in their trench across a rise in the centre of the table. The edges of the table represent the crest-line, and Boer figures can be fed on at the edges at random by the umpire. The table should include a good scattering of 'boulders' to provide cover for the infantry movement, whilst the umpire should introduce off-table artillery-fire against the British positions. The British player must simply hang on for a specified number of moves; if he's still there at the end, it is assumed that he is at last reinforced with mountain guns and artillery, the British have secured the position, and the entire Boer line has collapsed. The Relief of Ladysmith is therefore assured!

For those who prefer the smaller skirmish game, both battles offer the potential to recreate interesting incident; at Colenso, for example, the attempts to rescue the guns, or the skirmishing late in the day in the village itself. At Spioenkop the struggle for various sectors of the perimeter – for example the attack on the Lancashire Fusiliers trench, or on Colonel Hill's headquarters – offers a rare chance to pit British and Boer figures against one another at close quarters.

INDEX

(References to illustrations are shown in **bold**.)

Africans, black 8, 15
Afrikaners, origins of 7
Albrecht, Major 16
Aloe Knoll **42**, 64, **67**, 73, 77, **88**, **89**, 89

Barton, Major-General Geoffrey **37**, 37, 53
'Black Week' 7, 56
Bloemfontein 11, 85
Boer forces **8–9**, 12, 20, **23**, 39, 56–57, 85
    artillery 16, **22**, 33, **40**
    besiege Ladysmith 33, 39, 57, 83
    black Africans 15
    the British breakthrough 82, 83
    casualties 55, **72**, 78, 84
    at Cingolo 80
    at Colenso 39, **40**, 41–42, 49, 49(table),
        50, 51, 52–53, **54**, 54, 55, 80
    commanders 8, 18, 20
    commando system 13–15
    discipline 15
    dress 14, 16, **17**, 17, **19**, **20**
    at Elandslaagte Station 32
    Free State Artillery 16
    invade Natal 31–32, 33
    at Ntabamnyama 61
    officers 14–15, **19**
    organisation 14
    Police units 16
    route 83
    at Spioenkop 67–68, 68(table), 69, **72**,
        72, 73, 74, 75, **76**, 76, 77, 78
    Staatsartillerie 16
    strategy 12
    supplies 15
    tactics **22**
    uitlanders 17
    Vryheid Commando 38, 68
    weapons 17, **20**, 20
Boers, the 7, 8, 10, 11
Botha, Louis 33, 34, **38**, **39**, 80, 83
    background 38–39
    at Colenso 40–41, 42, 55
    at Spioenkop 69, 72, 73, 76
Brakfontein 60
British Colonial Office, the 10
British forces 12–13, 21, 27–28, 56, 60, **84**
    1st Royal Dragoons **26**
    2nd (Hildyard's) Brigade 37, 48, **51**, 51,
        53
        Devonshire Regiment 54, **62–63**
    4th (Lyttleton's) Brigade 37, 48, 52,
        53, 80
        King's Royal Rifle Corps 76–77, **77**
        Scottish Rifles 76, 77

5th (Hart's) Brigade 37, **48**, 48, 49–50,
    52, 53, **60**, 82
    Border Regiment 49, 50
    Connaught Rangers 49
    Royal Dublin Fusiliers 49, 51, 83
    Royal Inniskillin Fusiliers 49
5th (Warren's) Division 57
6th (Barton's) Brigade 34, 37, 42, 53,
    82–83
    Royal Irish Fusiliers **26**, 83
10th (Coke's) Brigade 66, 67
    Royal Lancaster Regiment **64**, 66
    Middlesex Regiment 76
    South Lancashire Regiment 66
11th (Woodgate's) Brigade 82
    Lancashire Fusiliers **65**, 66, 75–76, **80**
    artillery **24**, 25, 27, **28**, 37, 42, **44**, **45**,
        52, **53**, **55**, 55, **72**, **85**, **92**
        at Colenso 48–49, 49–50, 51–52, 53,
            54
    Bearer Company **83**
    breakthrough 80, 82–83
    casualties 35, 55, **73**, **74**, **75**, 78, 79,
        81, 84
    cavalry 25, **26**, 28, 38, 61, 83
        at Colenso 50, 52–53
    at Cingolo 80
    at Colenso 42, **44**, **45**, **48**, 48, 49(table),
        49–50, **50**, **51**, 52, 55
        artillery 48–49, 49–50, 51–52, 53, 54
        and Hlangwane ridge 52–53
        withdraw 53–54
    combat experience 21
    confidence 24
    at Elandslaagte Station 32
    fire discipline 21, 22
    Indian contingent 27–28
    in Ladysmith **28–29**, 33, 57, 84
        Devonshire Regiment 61
    lines of communication 33
    at Majuba 10
    Mournful Monday 14, **15**, **16**, 32
    in Natal 33
    at Ntabamnyama **60**, 61
    officers 25
    organisation 25, 27
    at Spioenkop **64**, **65**, 66–67, 68(table),
        72, **73**, 73–77, **74**, **75**, 77–78, **81**
        causes of failure 78–79
        entrench the summit 68–69
    staff officers 27
    tactics 21–22, 80
    transport 25, **27**
    uniforms **24**, 24–25, **26**
    at Vaalkranz ridge 79

volunteers 28, 66
    weapons 25
Buchanan-Riddell, Colonel 76, 77
Buller, General Sir Redvers (1839–1908)
    27, 33–34, **36**, 57
    background 36
    the breakthrough 80, 82
    at Colenso 42–44, 48, 51, 53, 54, 54–55
    criticism of 80
    criticism of Long 55, 56
    decision to attack at Colenso 35
    and Natal 31, 84
    plans 33–34, 60–61
    relief of Ladysmith 83–84
    response to Colenso 56
    at Spioenkop 64, 66, 74, 76, 79
    at Vaalkranz ridge 79
    and Warren 60, 61
Burger, Commandant Schalk **6**, 69
Butler, Sir William 12

Cape, the 7–8, 11
casualties 32, 35
    Colenso 55
    Ladysmith 84
    Spioenkop **72**, **73**, **74**, **75**, 78, **81**
    Vaalkranz ridge 79
chronology 91–92
Churchill, Winston (1874–1965) 33, 78
Cingolo 80
Clery, Lieutenant-General Sir Francis 34,
    36–37
Clouston Field of Rememberence 87
Coke, Colonel 66, 74, 77, 78
Coke, Major-General J Talbot **64**
Colenso 7, 33, 34, 39, 40, 80, **86**, 87
    battle of, 15th December 1899
        46–47(map)
    Boer forces **40**, 40–42, 49, 49(table), 50,
        51, 52–53, **54**, 54, 55
    British forces 42–44, **44**, **45**, **48**, 48–49,
        49(table), 49–50, **50**, **51**, 51–52,
        53–54
Colley, General Sir George 10
Conical Hill 64, **67**, 73, 75, **89**
Cooke, Colonel 77
Crofton, Colonel 74

dispositions
    Colenso 41–42, **46–47**(map)
    Ntabamnyama **58–59**(map)
    Spioenkop **58–59**(map), **70–71**(map)
Drakensberg mountains 12, 13, 31

Dundee 31, 32
Dundonald, Colonel Lord **38**, 38, 53, 61
Durban 8, 33
Dutch East India Company, the 7

Elandslaagte 83
Elandslaagte Station, battle of, 21st
    October 1899 32
Estcourt 33

Fort Wylie 40, 41, **44**, 87
Frere 34

Gatacre, Lieutenant-General 35
Great Britain 7, 7–8, 10, 56
    and the Boers 7, 8, 11, 20
Great Trek, the 8
Green Hill 64
Groenkop 64

Hamilton, Major-General Ian 32
Hart, Major-General Alan Fitzroy **36**, 37,
    50–51
Hart's Hill 82, 83–84
Hildyard, Major-General H J T **37**, 37
Hill, Colonel 77
Hlangwane ridge 41–42, 44, 48, 52–53, 80

Jameson, Dr Leander Starr 11
Jameson Raid, the, 1895 10–11
Johannesburg 10
Joubert, General Piet **8**, **10**, 12, 31, 33, 38

Kimberley 10, 12, 34
Kock, Commandant J H M **21**
Kruger, President Paul **7**, 10, 11, 85

Ladysmith **14**, 31, 34, 86–87
    battle of, 30th October 1899 **15**, 32
    Boer advance on 32–33
    relief of 83–84
    siege of 39, 57
Long, Colonel Charles **37**, 37, 48, 55, 56
Lyttleton, Major-General Neville **37**, 37, 76

Mafikeng 12
Magersfontein heights 7, 35
Majuba, battle of, 26th February 1881 10,
    12, 31
Methuen, Lord 35
Meyer, Lieutenant Lukas 32, 38
Milner, Sir Alfred 11
Mount Alice 60, **92**
Mournful Monday **14**, **15**, **16**, 32

Natal 8, 11, 12, **31**(map), 31, 84
Naval Gun Hill **50**, 51
Newcastle 31, 32
Nicholson's Nek, battle of, 30th October
    1899 32
Ntabamnyama **42**
    attack on, 19/20th January 1900
    58–59(map), **60**, 61

Orange Free State, the 8, 11
Orange River 8

Paadeberg 84
Parsons, Lieutenant-Colonel L W 49–50
Penn-Symons, General 12, 31, 32
Pepworth, battle of, 30th October 1899 32
Pietermaritzburg 33
Pieter's Hill 82–83, 83–84
Platrand 57, **62–63**
Port Natal (Durban) 8
Potgeiter's Drift 34, 60
Pretoria 85
Prinsloo, Commandant Hendrik 69, 72

Railway Hill 83, 83–84
Rhodes, Cecil 10, 11, 34
Rietfontein 32
Roberts, Lord Frederick (1832–1914) 56,
    79, 84, 84–85
Roberts, Lieutenant Freddie **52**, 53, 55

Schofield, Captain 53, 55
slavery 8
South Africa 7, **18**(map)
South African Republic. *see* Transvaal, the
Spioenkop **42**, **57**, 61, 64, **67**, **87**, **88**, **89**, 89
    battle of, 24th January 1900
    58–59(map), **69**, **70–71** (map)

Boer forces 67–68, 68(table), 69, **72**,
    72, 73, 74, 75, **76**, 76, 77, 78
British forces **64**, **65**, 66–67, 68
    (table), 68–69, 72, **73**, 73–77, **74**,
    75, 77–78, **81**
Stormberg railway junction 7, 35

Talana Hill 32
theatre of operations **18** (map), **31**
    (map), **43** (map), **82** (map)
Thorneycroft, Colonel Alec **66**, 67, 74, 75,
    76, 78
Thukela heights **42**, **57**, 83, 89
Thukela River 31, 34, **40**, 40, **41**, **44**,
    50–51, **84**, 89
trains, armoured **25**, 33
Transvaal, the 8, 10, 11, 16
Trichardt's Drift 60, 61, 89
Tweede Vryheidsoorlog 11
Twin Peaks **57**, 64, **67**, 76–77, **88**, 89

uitlanders 10, 11, 17, 28

Vaalkranz ridge 79, **85**

Wagon Hill 57, **62–63**
Warren, Lieutenant-General Sir Charles
    44, **57**, 57, 60, 61, 64, 69, 74, 75, 76, 79
weapons 22
    Boer forces 17, **20**, 20
    British forces 25
    machine guns 25
White, Lieutenant-General Sir George **13**,
    27, 31, 32, 33, 34, 44, 56, 83
Willow Grange 33
Witwatersrand 10
Wolseley, Sir Garnett (1823–1913) 12, 36
Woodgate, Major-General E R P 66, 67,
    68, 69, 72, 74
Wynne's Hill 82, 83–84

Yule, Major-General 32

Zulus, the 10, 31